PUFF THE MAGIC DRAGON
and 54 Other All-Time Children's Favorites

Arranged by Carol Klose and Edwin McLean

ISBN 978-1-57560-146-5

Visit our website at
www.cherrylane.com

CONTENTS

4 Alouette

6 A-Tisket A-Tasket

8 The Bear Went Over the Mountain

10 Blow the Man Down

12 Brahms' Lullaby

14 Canon in D (Pachelbel Canon)

20 Conjunction Junction

17 Dance Little Bird (The Chicken Dance)

22 Dance of the Hours

28 Dance of the Sugar Plum Fairy

30 Day-O (The Banana Boat Song)

34 Deck the Halls

36 Did You Ever See a Lassie?

38 Eensy Weensy Spider

40 The Farmer in the Dell

42 Für Elise

25 The Great American Melting Pot

44 The Happy Farmer

46 Hark! The Herald Angels Sing

48 How 'Bout That

58 If You're Happy and You Know It

54 I'm Just a Bill

60 It's Raining, It's Pouring

56 I've Been Working on the Railroad

62 Jingle Bells

64 John Jacob Jingleheimer Schmidt

66 Joy to the World

68 Leaving on a Jet Plane

72 London Bridge Is Falling Down

74 Michael Finnegan

76 Minuet in G

78 The Muffin Man

80 The Mulberry Bush

82 Oh Where, Oh Where Has My Little Dog Gone

84 Old MacDonald Had a Farm

86 Over the River and Through the Woods

51 Pokémon Theme

88 Pomp and Circumstance

90 Pop Goes the Weasel

92 Puff the Magic Dragon

94 She'll Be Comin' 'Round the Mountain

96 Silent Night

98 Sing a Song of Sixpence

100 The Skaters' Waltz

102 Skip to My Lou

104 Someday Out of the Blue (Theme from *El Dorado*)

108 "Surprise" Symphony

110 Ten Little Indians

112 Thank You Very Much

116 There Was an Old Woman Who Lived in a Shoe

118 This Old Man

120 Twinkle, Twinkle Little Star

122 We Wish You a Merry Christmas

124 When You Believe (from *The Prince Of Egypt*)

126 William Tell Overture

A-Tisket A-Tasket

Traditional

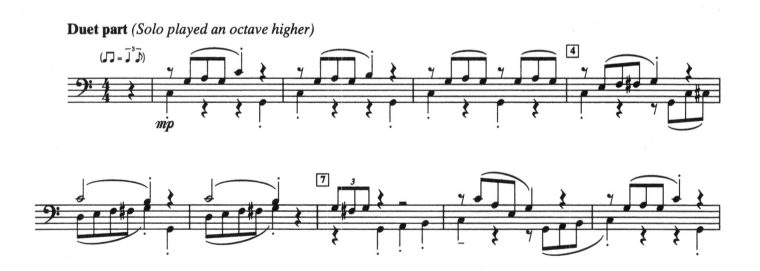

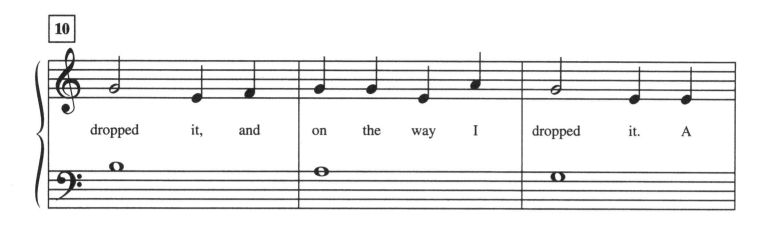

dropped it, and on the way I dropped it. A

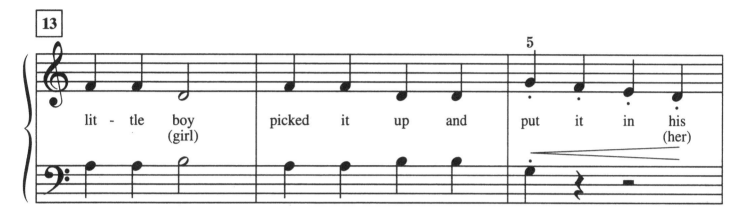

lit - tle boy (girl) picked it up and put it in his (her)

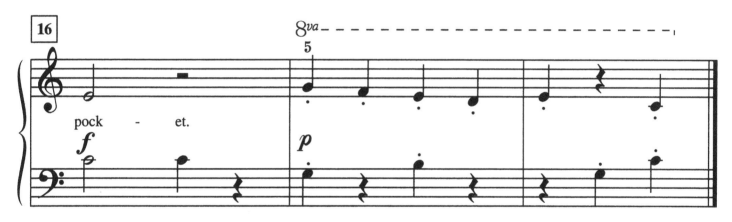

pock - et.

5

Alouette

Traditional

The Bear Went Over the Mountain

Not too fast, with a lumbering air

Lyrics under staff:
The bear went o-ver the moun-
saw an-oth-er moun-

tain, the bear went o-ver the mountain, he saw an-oth-er moun-

tain. The bear went o-ver the
tain. He saw an-oth-er

Duet part *(Solo played an octave higher)*

Blow the Man Down

Traditional Sea Chantey

Heartily, with a fast Waltz beat

Duet part (*Solo played an octave higher*)

Brahms' Lullaby

By Johannes Brahms

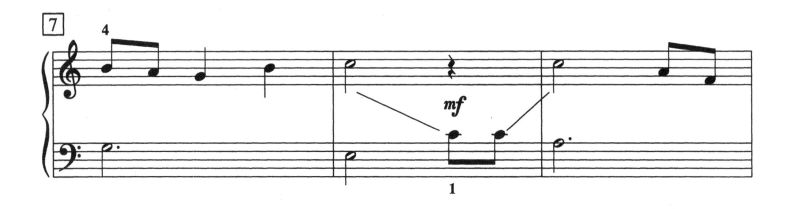

Duet part *(Solo played an octave higher)*

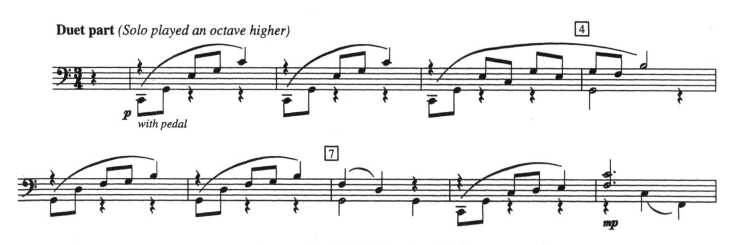

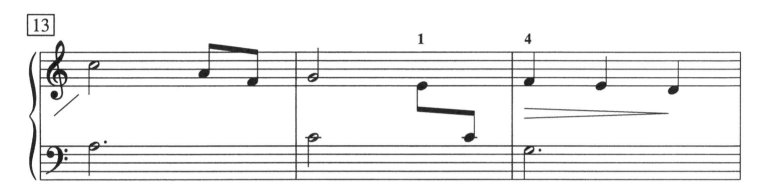

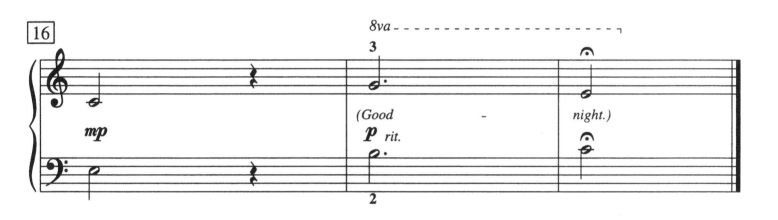

Canon in D
(Pachelbel Canon)

By Johann Pachelbel

Gently

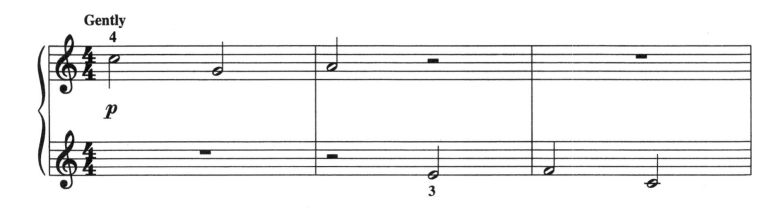

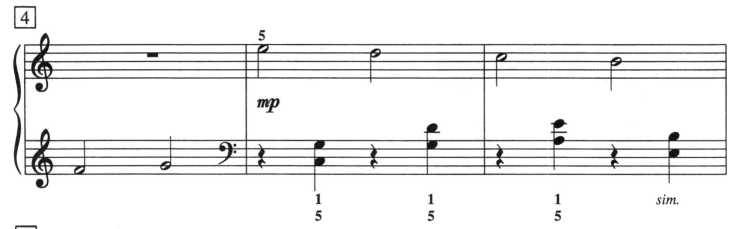

Duet part (*Solo played an octave higher*)

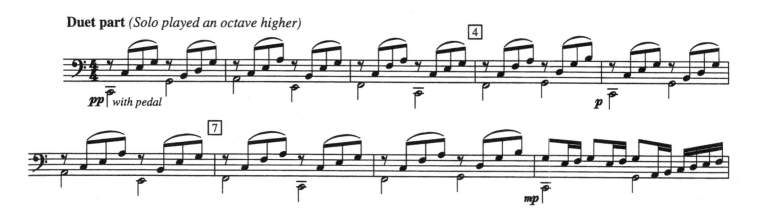

Dance Little Bird
(The Chicken Dance)

By Terry Rendall and Werner Thomas

Medium polka beat, in "2"

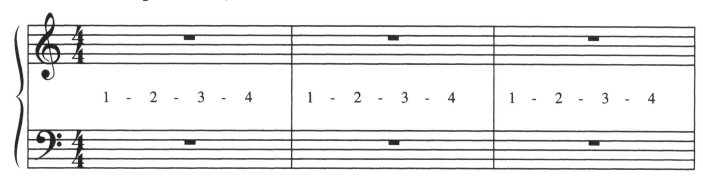

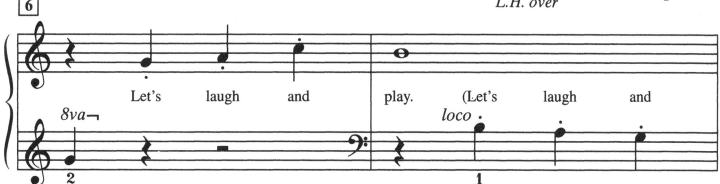

Duet Part *(Solo played an octave higher)*

Got a prob - lem? Here's a cure. (We got the loco

cure.) Do the chick - en dance;

L.H. over

make you hap - py for sure.

f

sfz

mf

19

Conjunction Junction

Words and Music by
Bob Dorough

Begin here for solo

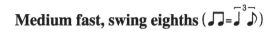

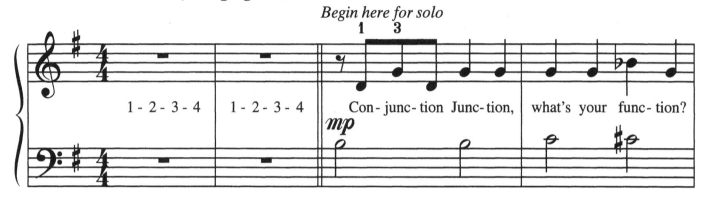

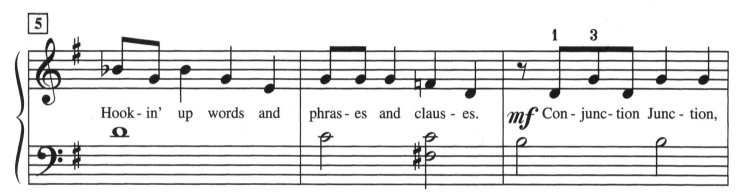

Duet Part (*Solo played an octave higher*)

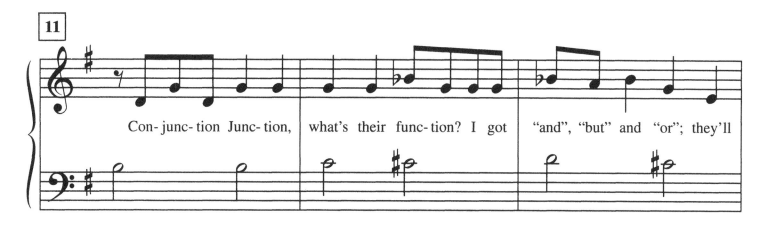

Con- junc-tion Junc-tion, what's their func-tion? I got "and", "but" and "or"; they'll

get you pret-ty far.— Con- junc-tion Junc-tion, what's your func-tion? I'm gonna

get you there if you're ver-y care-ful.

Dance of the Hours
from LA GIOCONDA

By A. Ponchielli

Moderately, delicately

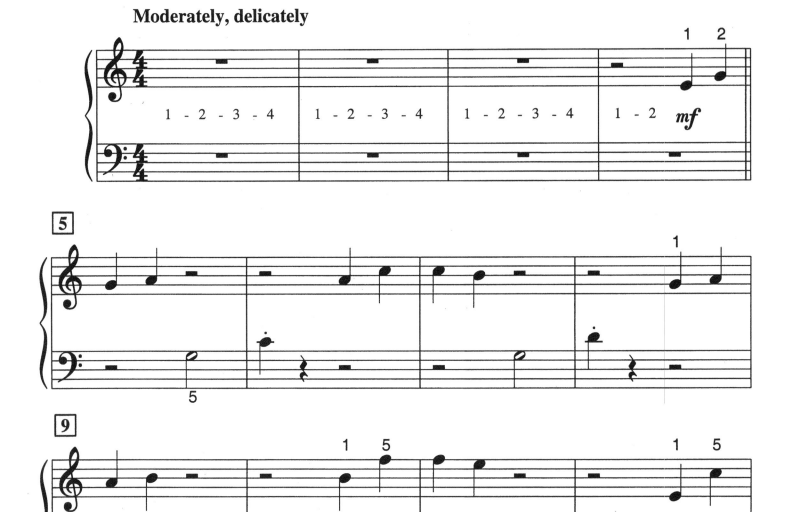

Duet Part (*Solo played an octave higher*)

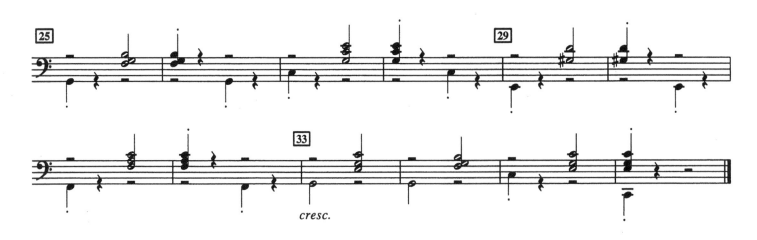

The Great American Melting Pot

Words and Music by
Lynn Ahrens

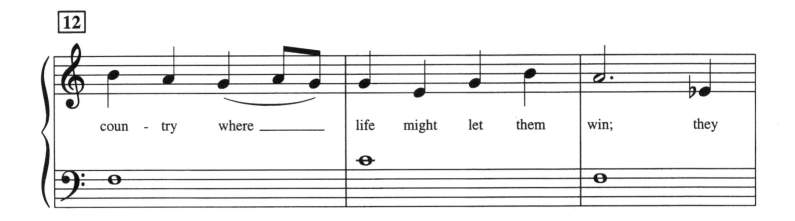

coun - try where _____ life might let them win; they

paid the fare to A - mer - i - ca and there they melt - ed

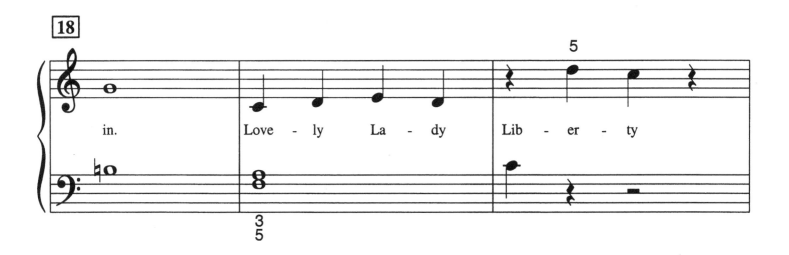

in. Love - ly La - dy Lib - er - ty

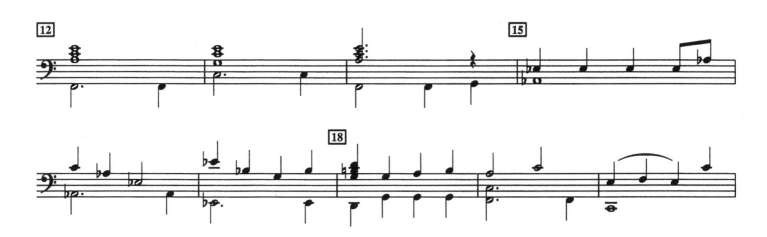

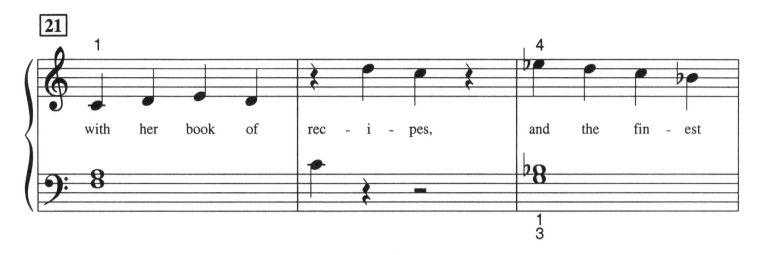

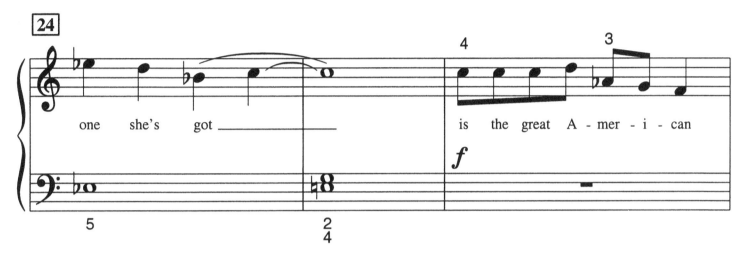

Dance of the Sugar Plum Fairy

from THE NUTCRACKER

By Pyotr Il'yich Tchaikovsky

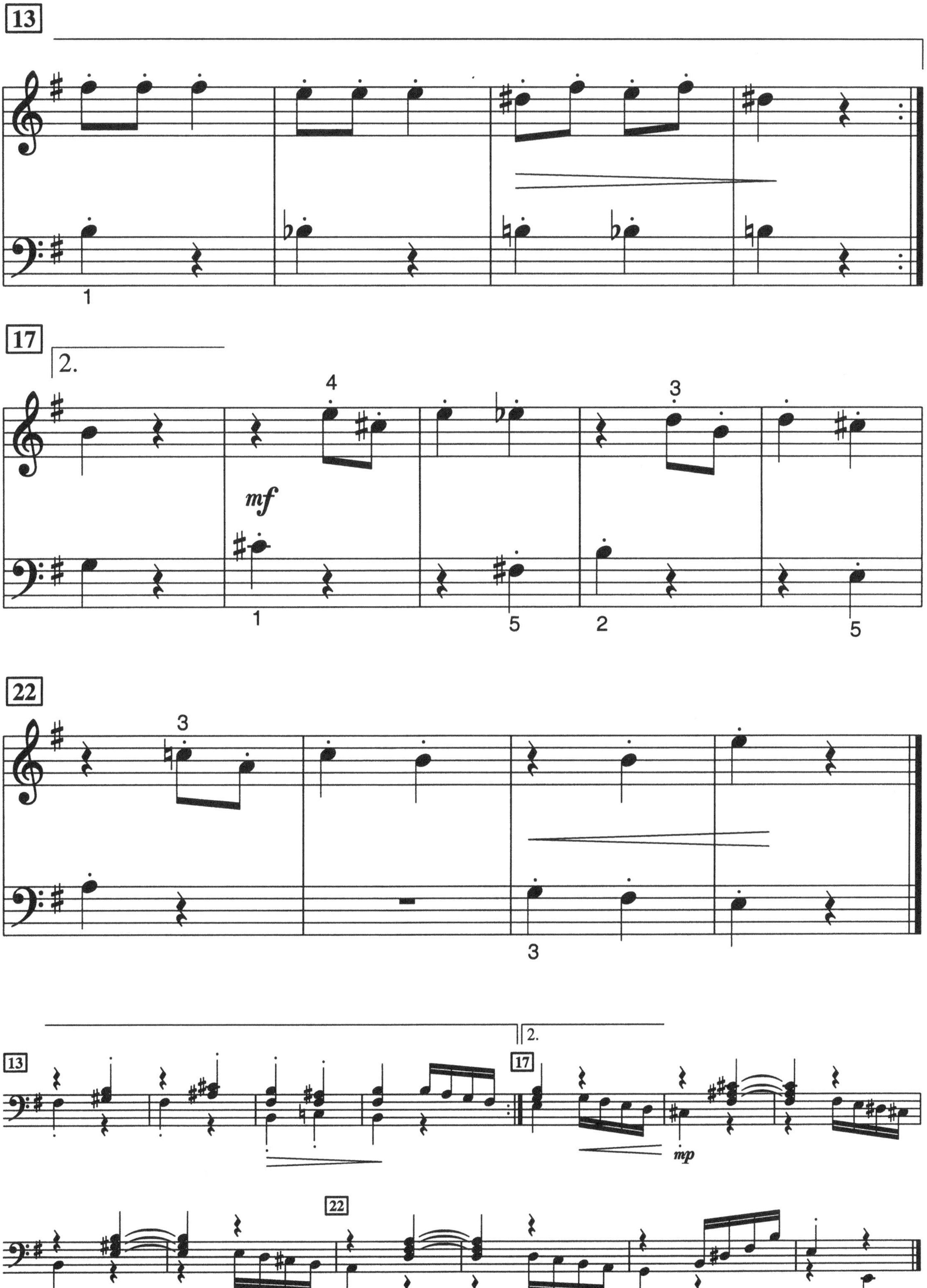
13
17
2.
4
3
mf
22
3
13
2.
17
mp
22

Day-O
(The Banana Boat Song)

Words and Music by
Irving Burgie and William Attaway

Medium fast, with a steady beat

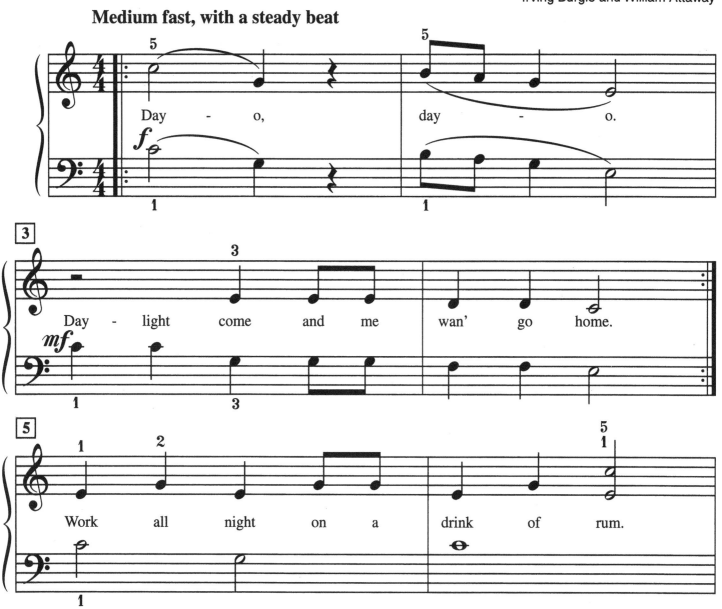

Day - o,   day - o.

Day - light   come   and   me   wan'   go   home.

Work   all   night   on   a   drink   of   rum.

Duet Part (*Solo played an octave higher*)

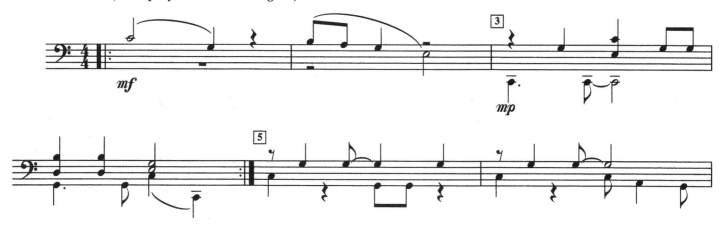

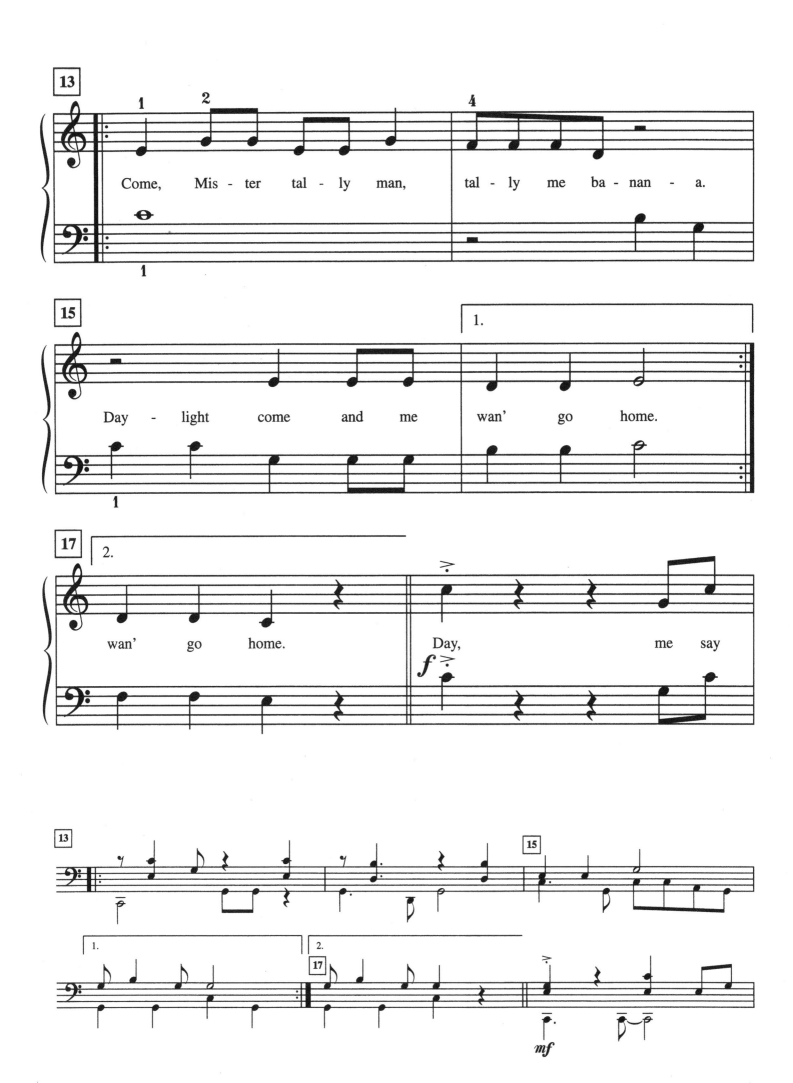

Come, Mis - ter tal - ly man, tal - ly me ba - nan - a.

Day - light come and me wan' go home.

wan' go home. Day, me say

Deck the Halls

Traditional Welsh Carol

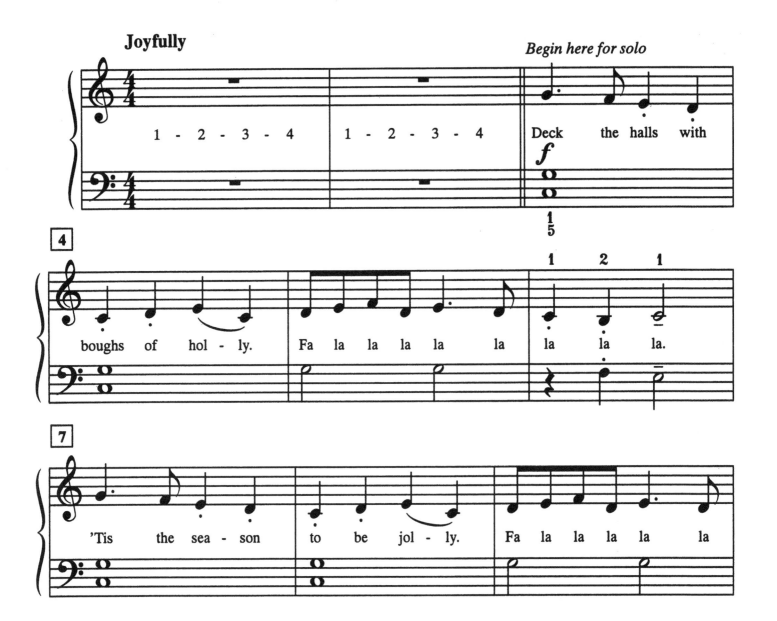

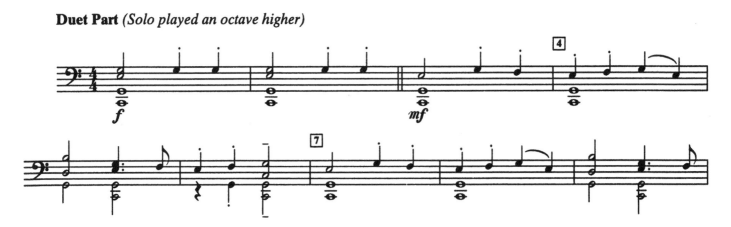

Duet Part *(Solo played an octave higher)*

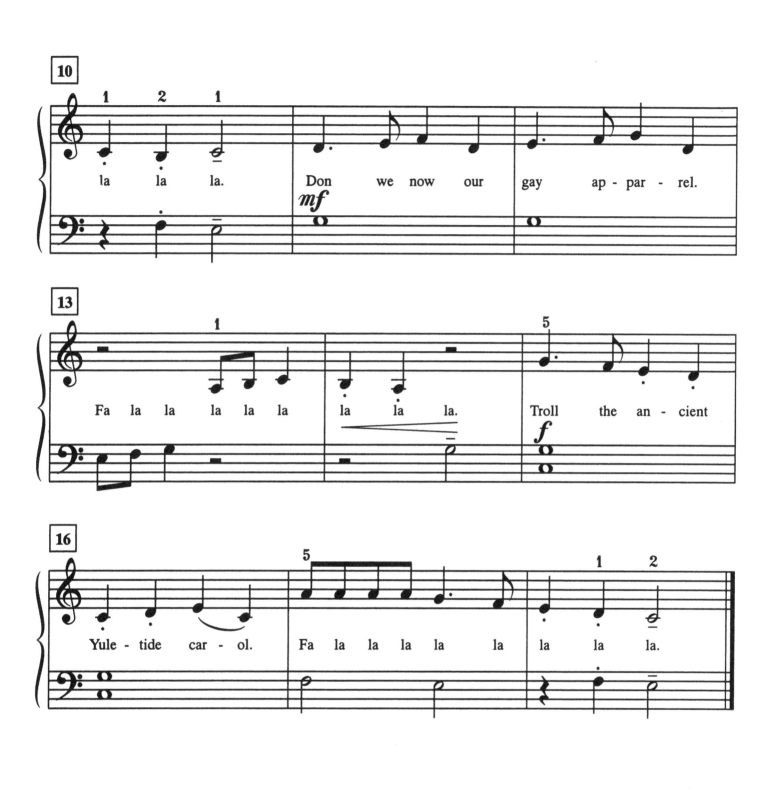

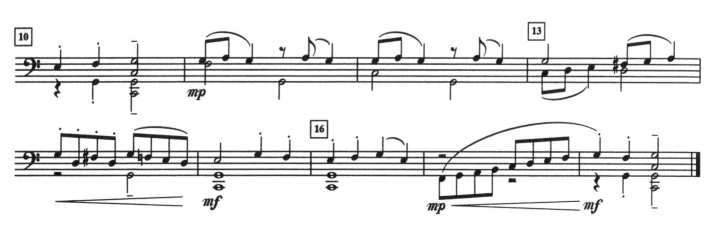

Did You Ever See a Lassie?

Traditional

Lilting, rather fast

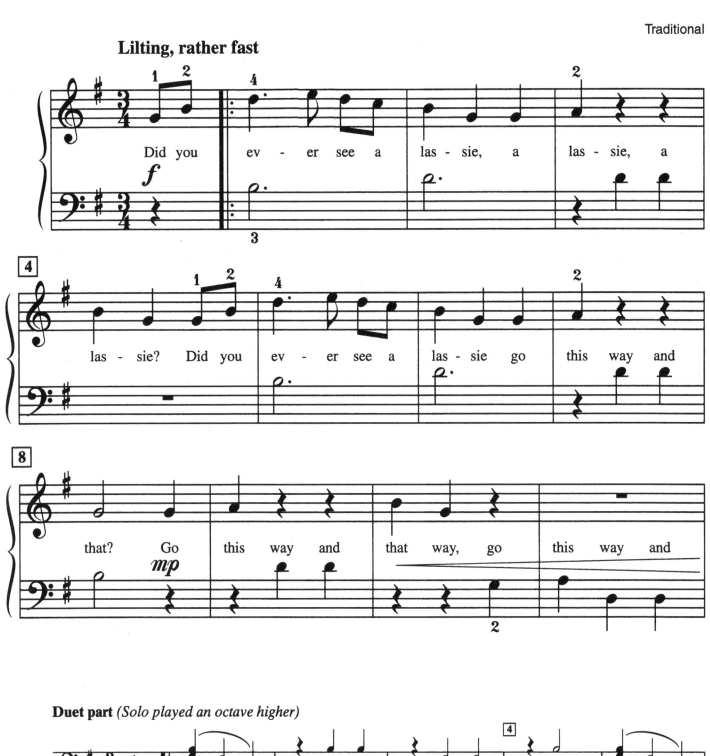

Did you ev - er see a las - sie, a las - sie, a las - sie? Did you ev - er see a las - sie go this way and that? Go this way and that way, go this way and

Duet part *(Solo played an octave higher)*

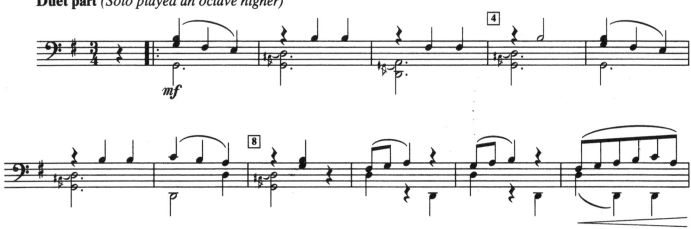

Eensy Weensy Spider

Traditional

Duet Part *(Solo played an octave higher)*

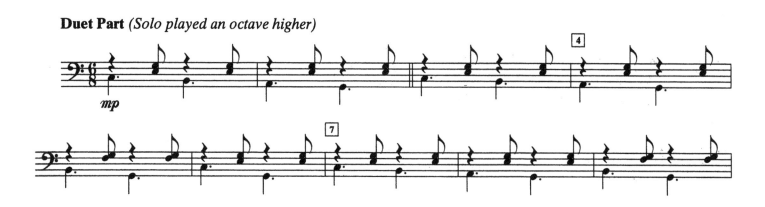

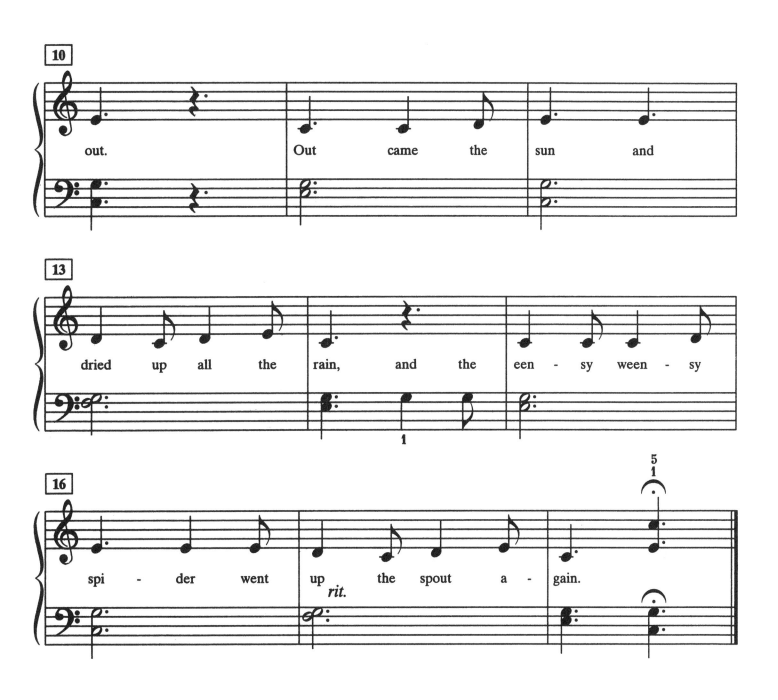

The Farmer in the Dell

Traditional

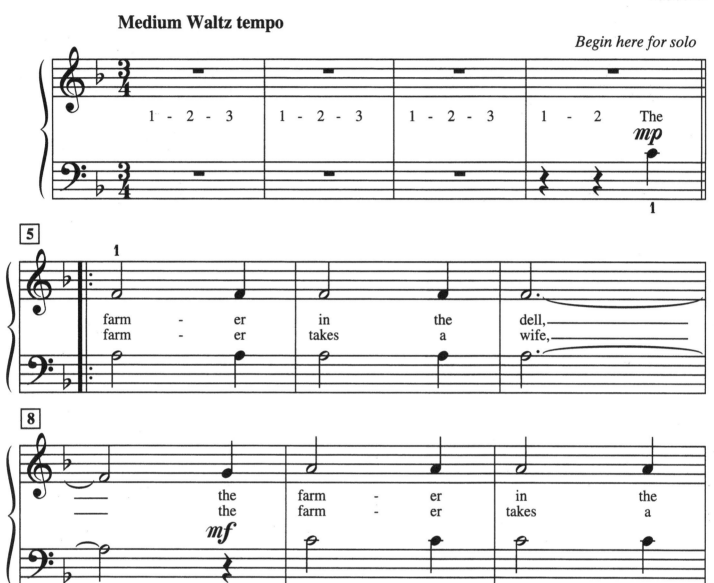

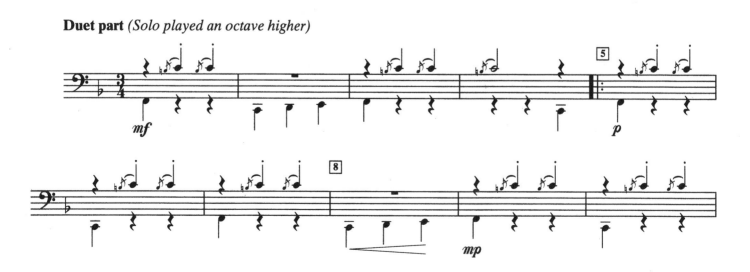

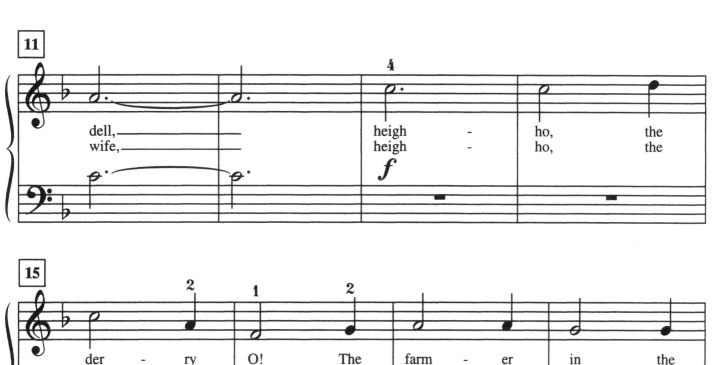

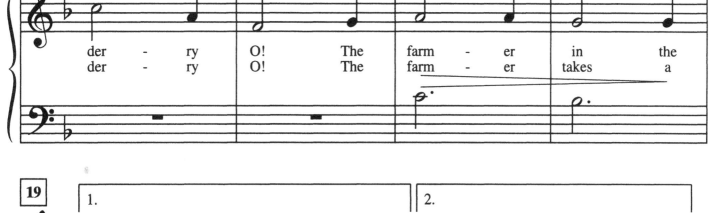

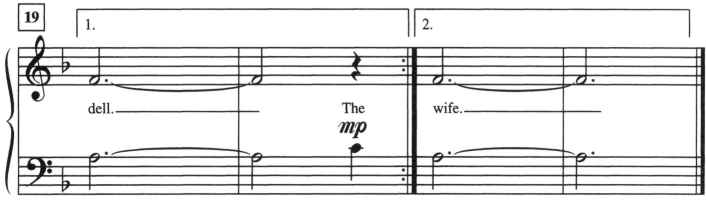

41

Für Elise

By Ludwig van Beethoven

Moderately slow, with expression

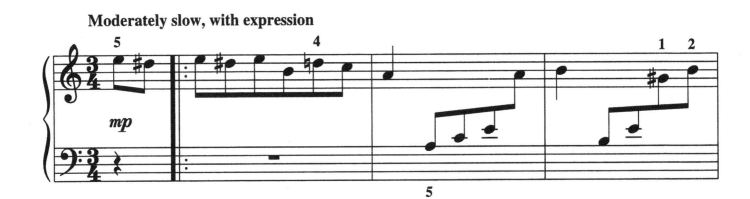

Duet part (*Solo played an octave higher*)

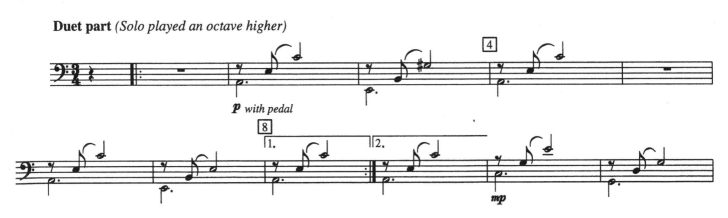

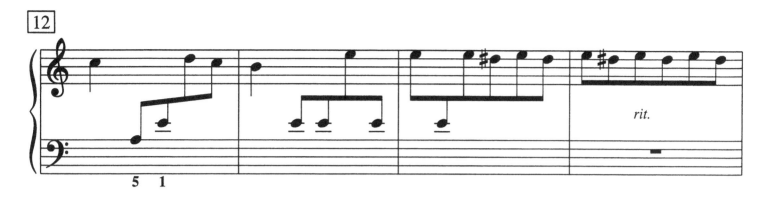

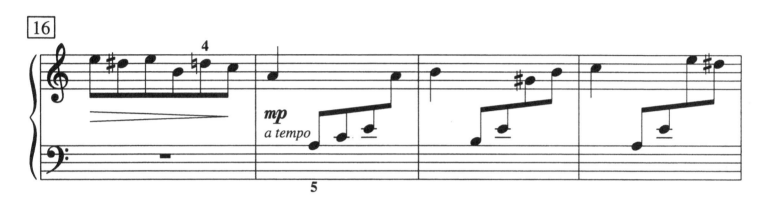

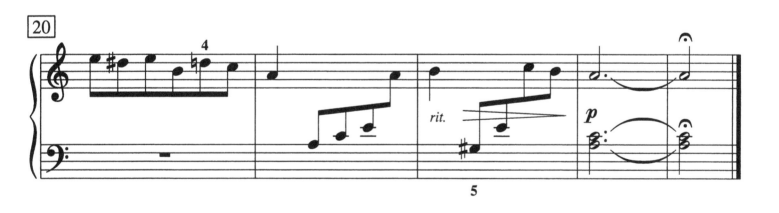

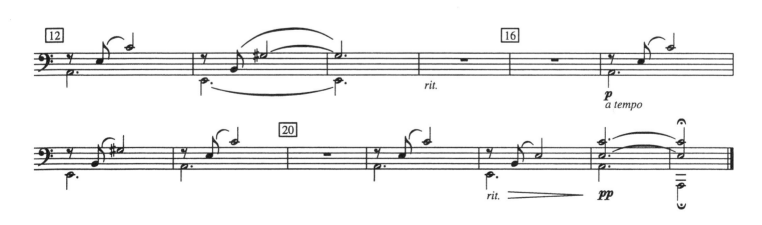

43

The Happy Farmer
from ALBUM FUR DIE JUGEND (ALBUM FOR THE YOUNG)

By Robert Schumann

Duet Part *(Solo played an octave higher)*

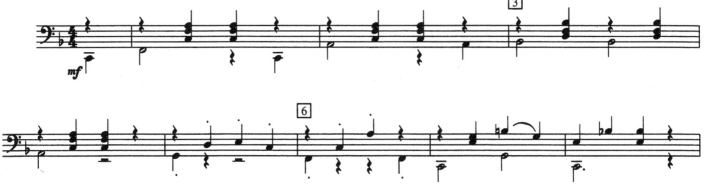

Hark! The Herald Angels Sing

Words by Charles Wesley
Altered by George Whitefield

Music by Felix Mendelssohn-Bartholdy
Arranged by William H. Cummings

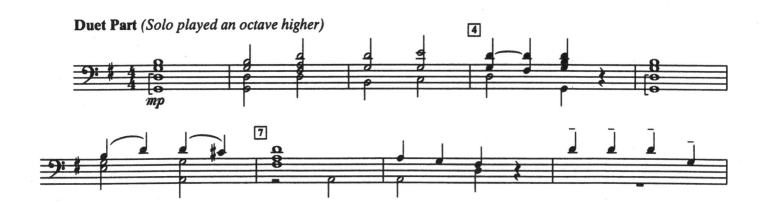

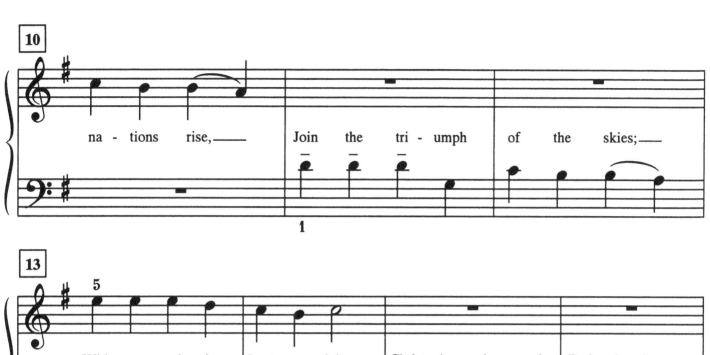

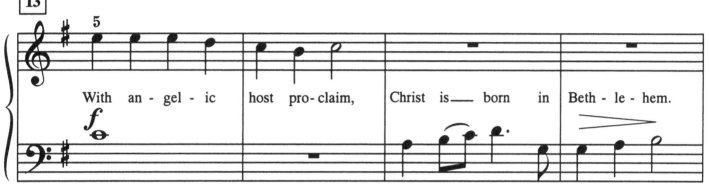

How 'Bout That

Theme from the Television Series HOW 'BOUT THAT

Words and Music by
Tim Noah

Moderately fast Rock beat

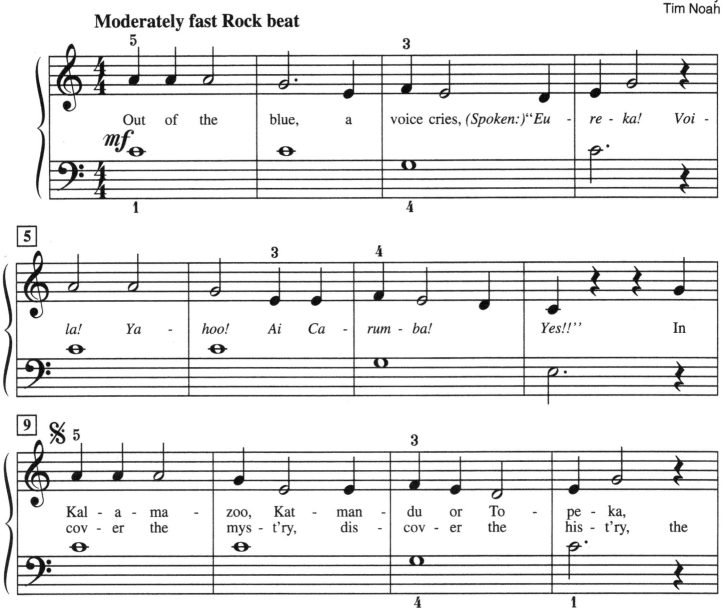

Duet Part *(Solo played an octave higher)*

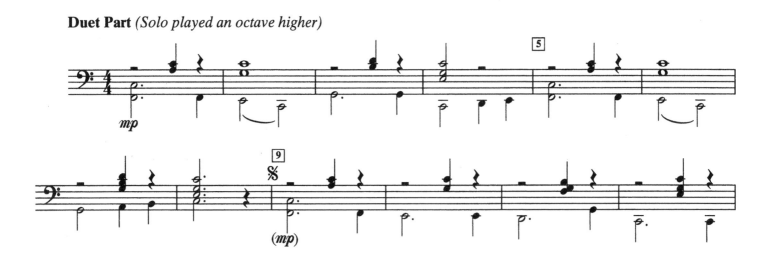

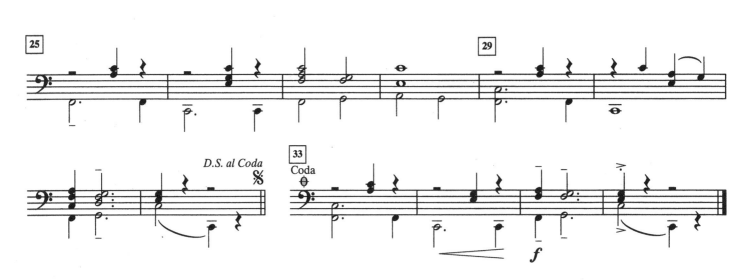

Pokémon Theme

Words and Music by
T. Loeffler and J. Siegler

Medium fast, with a steady beat

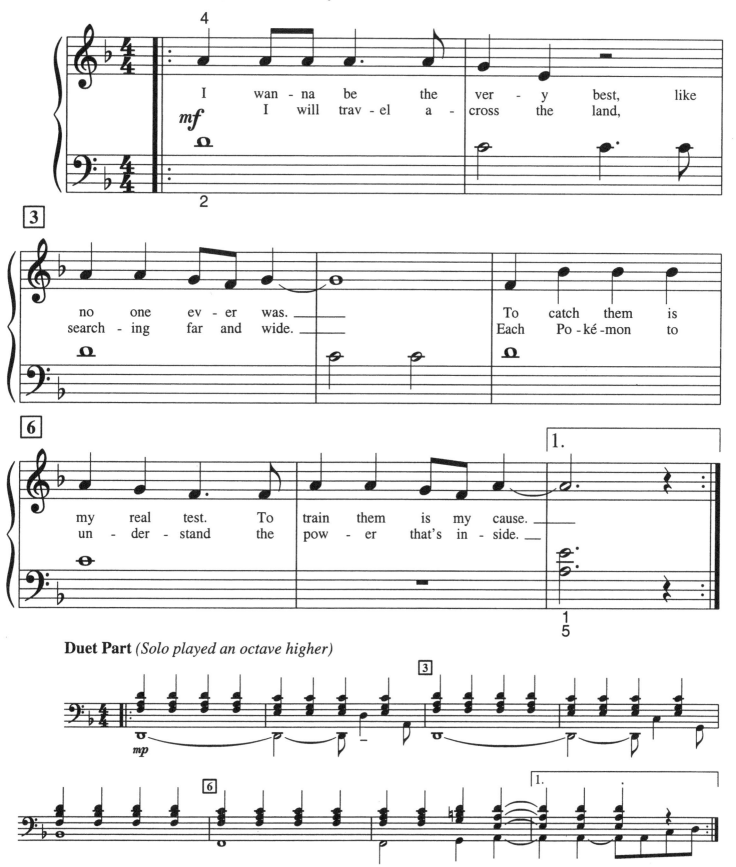

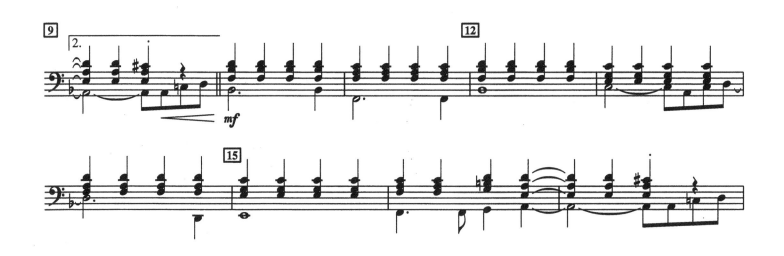

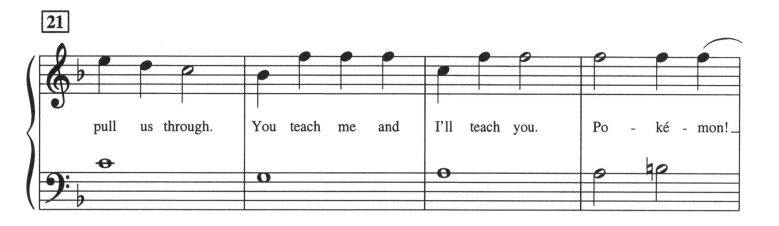

I'm Just a Bill

Words and Music by
Dave Frishberg

Medium fast, in "2"

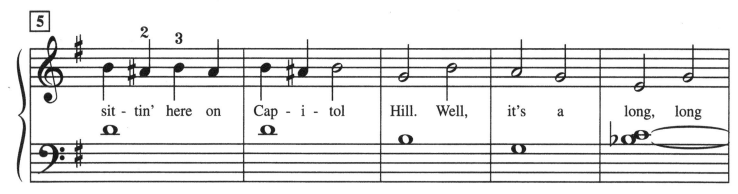

Duet Part *(Solo played an octave higher)*

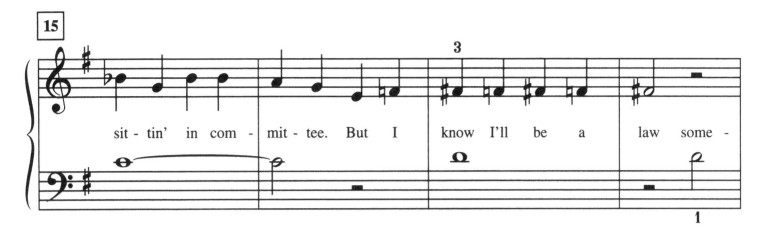

sit - tin' in com - mit - tee. But I know I'll be a law some -

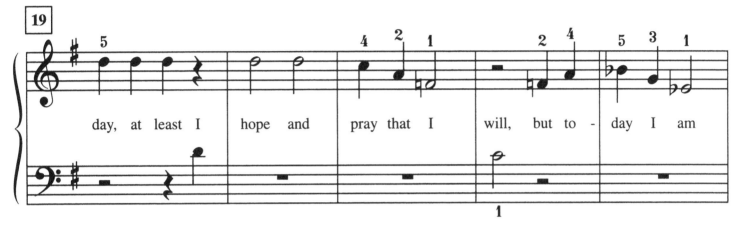

day, at least I hope and pray that I will, but to - day I am

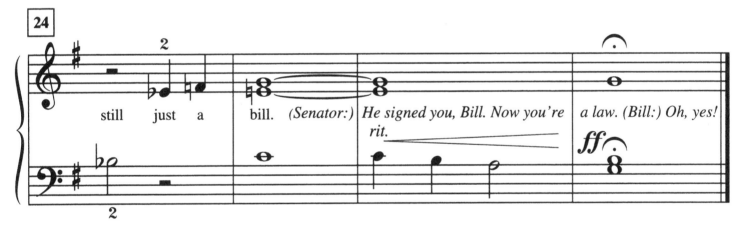

still just a bill. *(Senator:)* *He signed you, Bill. Now you're* *a law. (Bill:) Oh, yes!*
rit.

I've Been Working on the Railroad

American Folksong

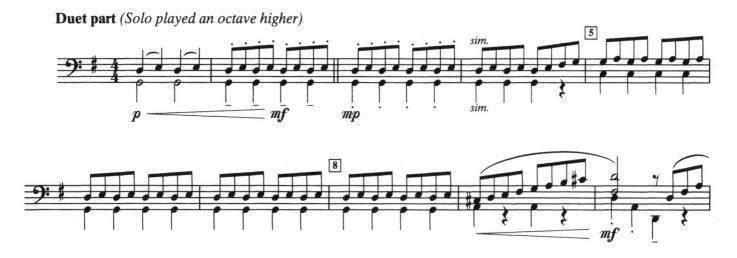

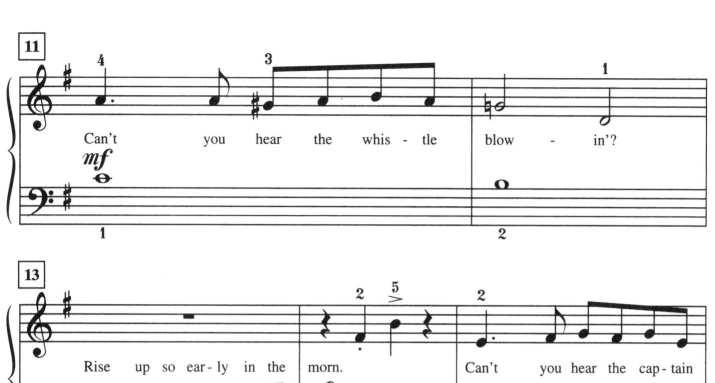

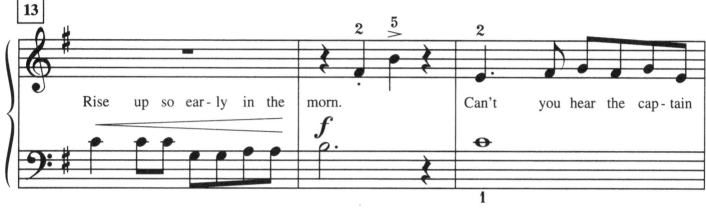

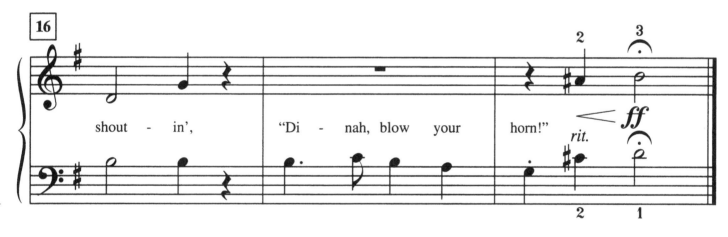

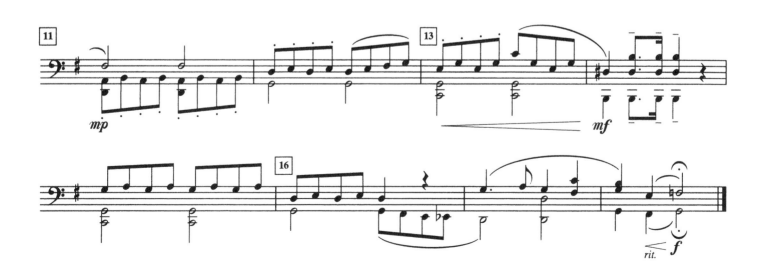

If You're Happy and You Know It

Words and Music by
L. Smith

Duet Part *(Solo played an octave higher)*

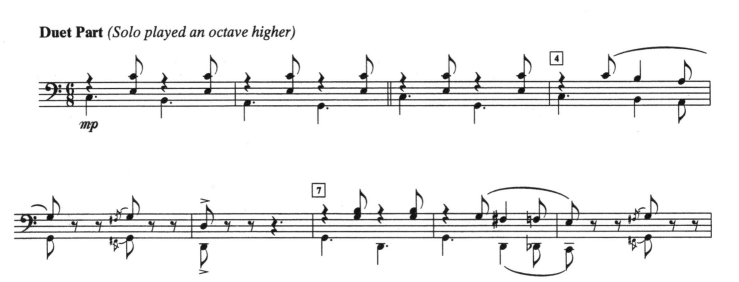

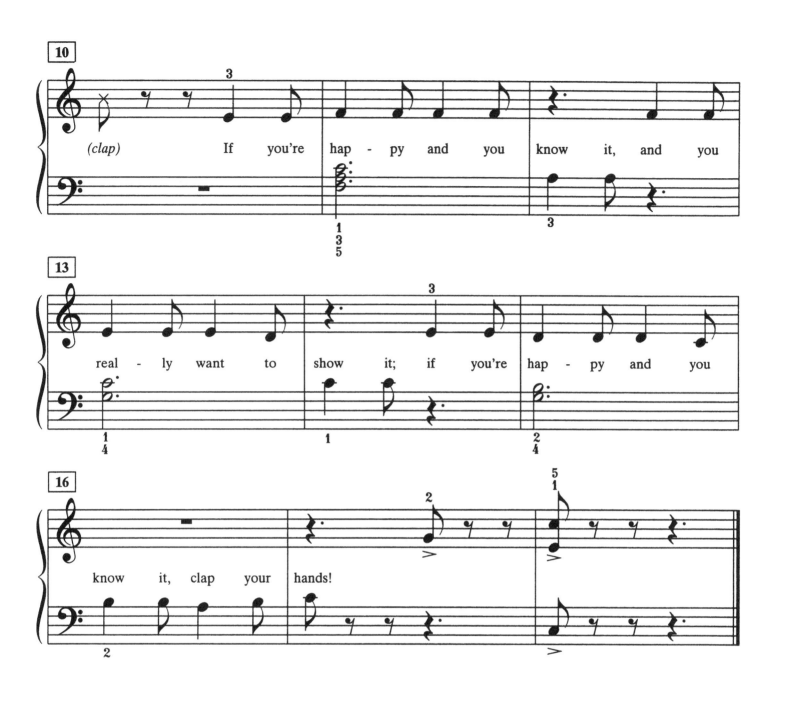

It's Raining, It's Pouring

Traditional

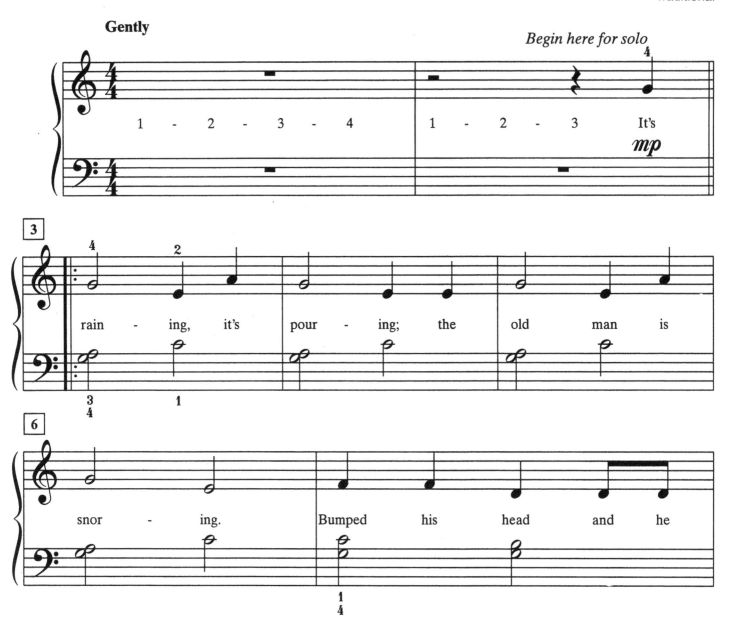

Duet Part *(Solo played an octave higher)*

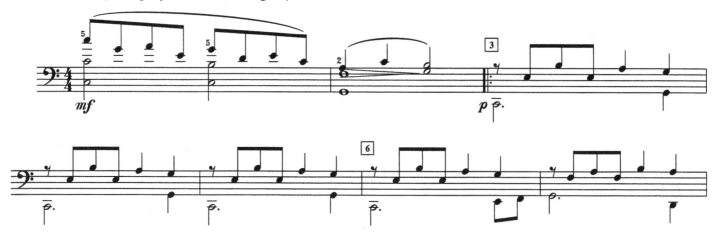

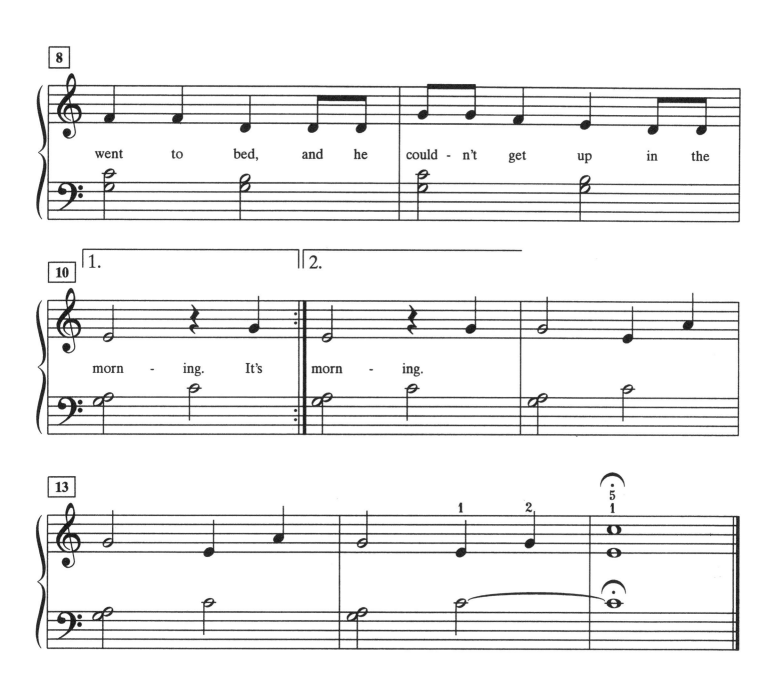

went to bed, and he could - n't get up in the morn - ing. It's morn - ing.

61

Jingle Bells

Words and Music by
J. Pierpont

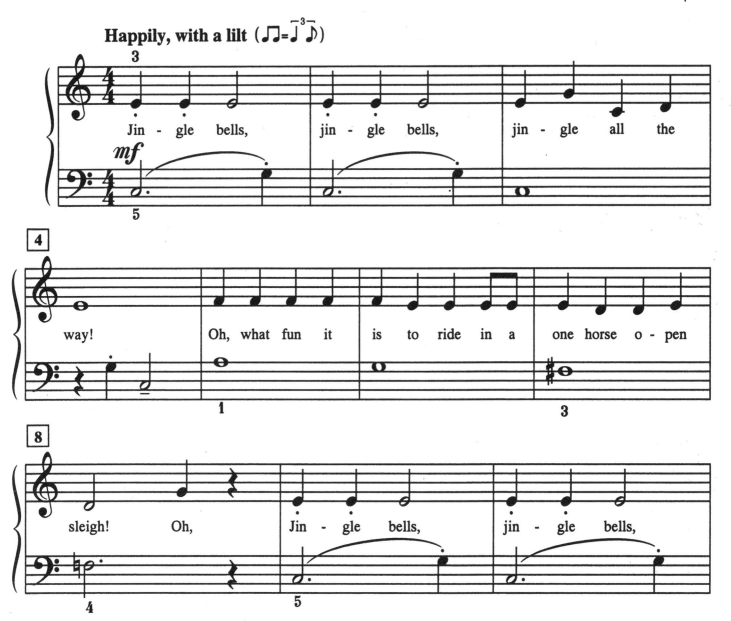

Duet Part *(Solo played an octave higher)*

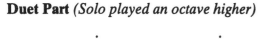

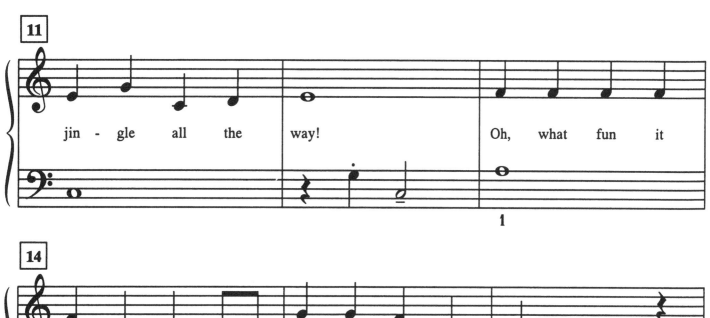

jin - gle all the way! Oh, what fun it

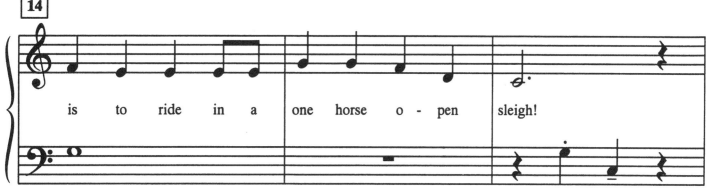

is to ride in a one horse o - pen sleigh!

John Jacob Jingleheimer Schmidt

Traditional

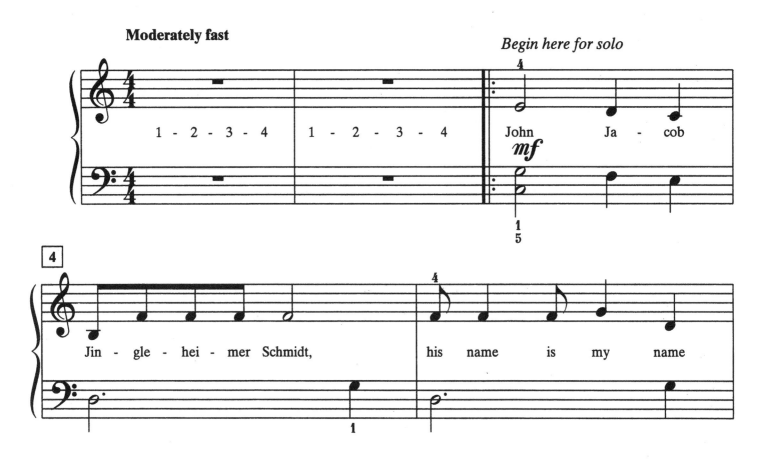

Duet Part (*Solo played an octave higher*)

Joy to the World

Words by Isaac Watts

Music by George Frideric Handel
Arranged by Lowell Mason

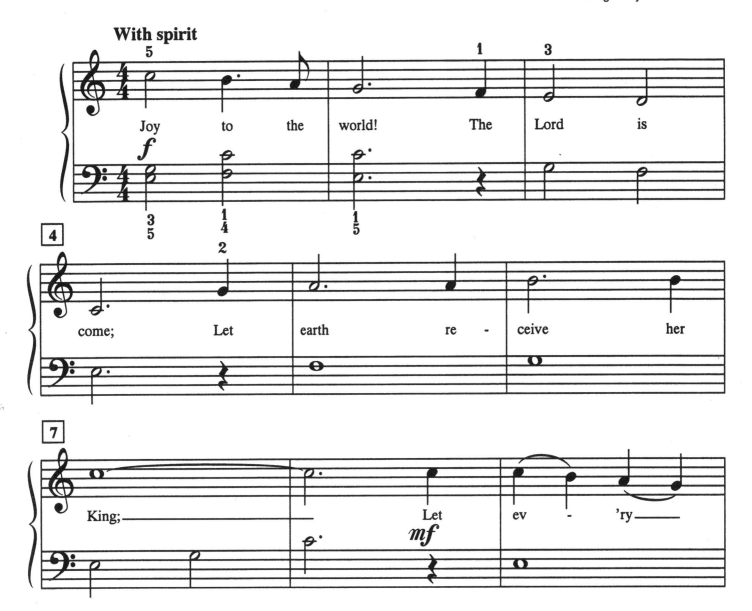

Duet Part *(Solo played an octave higher)*

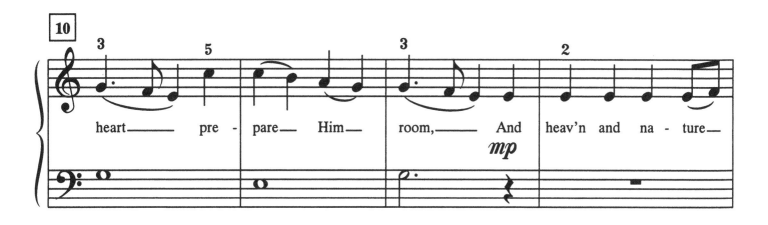

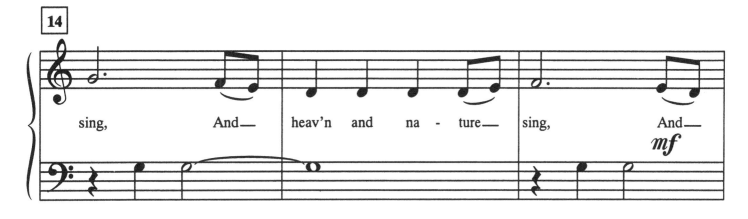

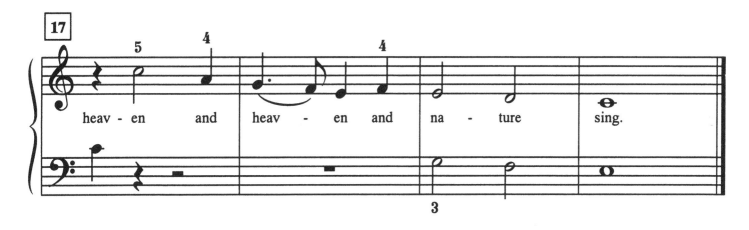

Leaving on a Jet Plane

Words and Music by
John Denver

Moderately

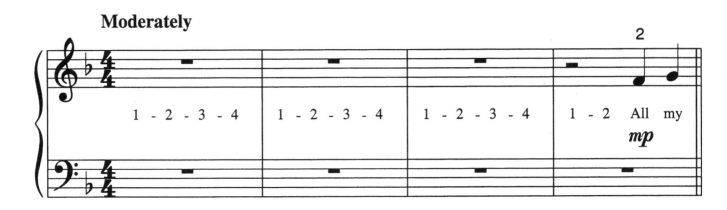

Duet Part (*Solo played an octave higher*)

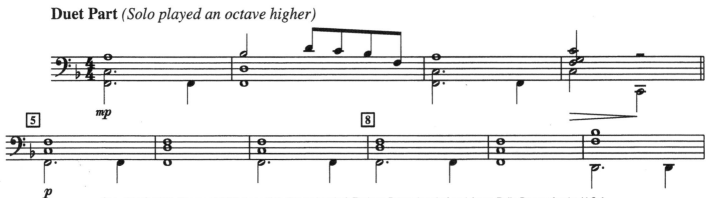

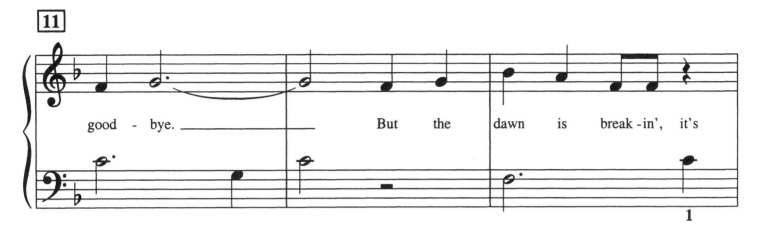

good - bye. _____ But the dawn is break -in', it's

ear - ly morn. The tax - i's wait - in', he's

blow -in' his horn. Al - read - y I'm so lone - some I could

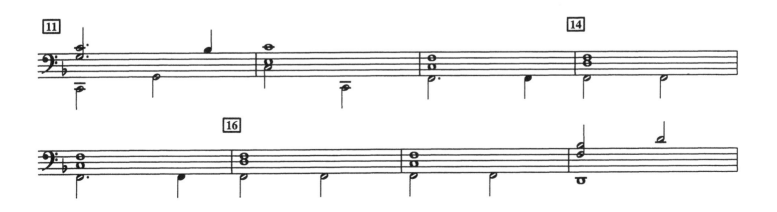

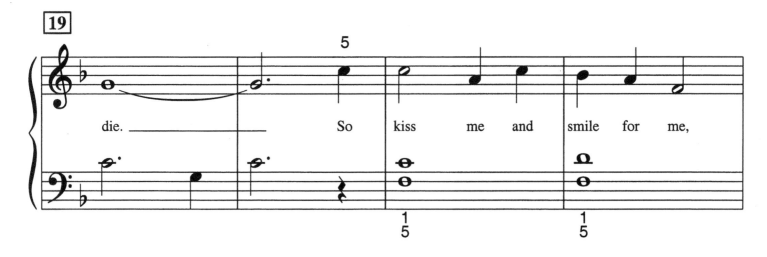

die. _____ So kiss me and smile for me,

tell me that you'll wait for me, hold me like you'll

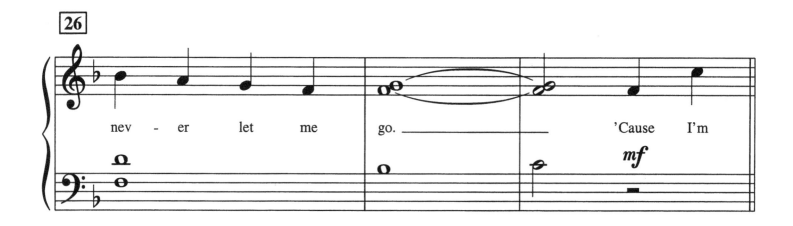

nev - er let me go. _____ 'Cause I'm

mf

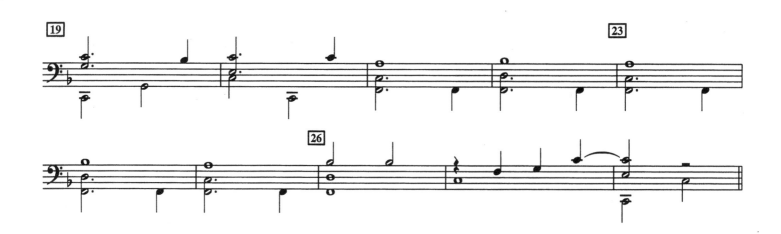

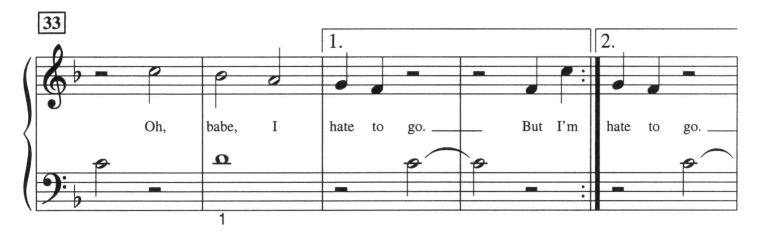

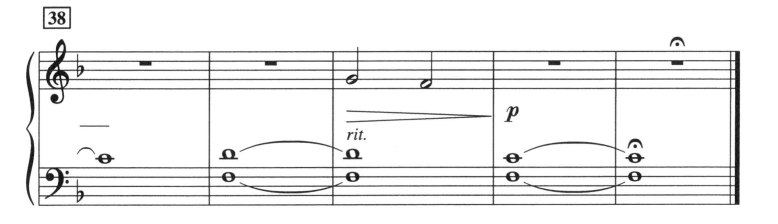

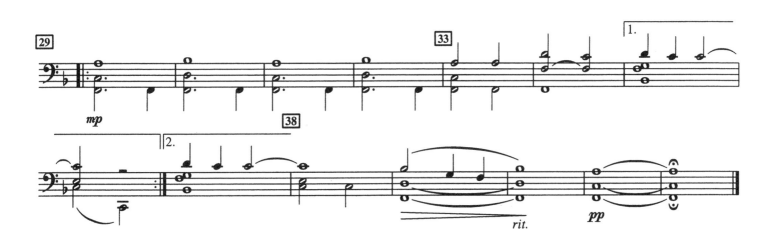

71

London Bridge Is Falling Down

Traditional

Moderately

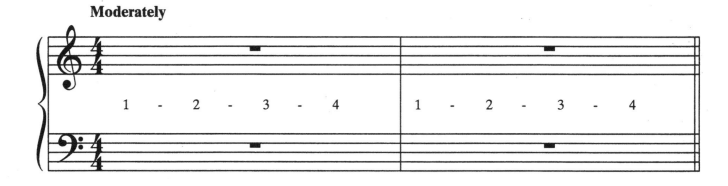

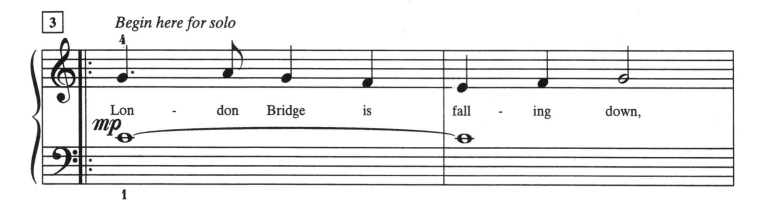

Duet Part *(Solo played an octave higher)*

fall - ing down, fall - ing down.

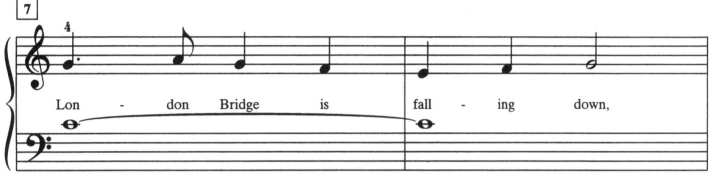

Lon - don Bridge is fall - ing down,

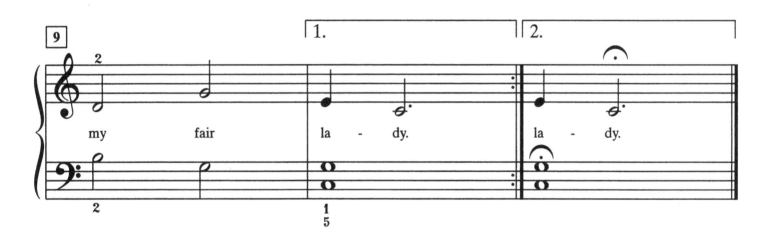

my fair la - dy. la - dy.

Michael Finnegan

Traditional

Moderately, with a steady beat

Duet part *(Solo played an octave higher)*

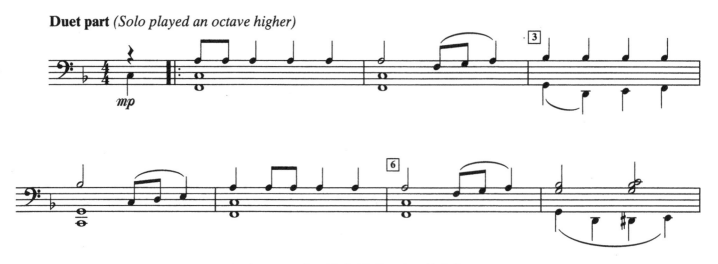

Minuet in G
from the ANNA MAGDALENA NOTEBOOK (originally for keyboard)

By Johann Sebastian Bach

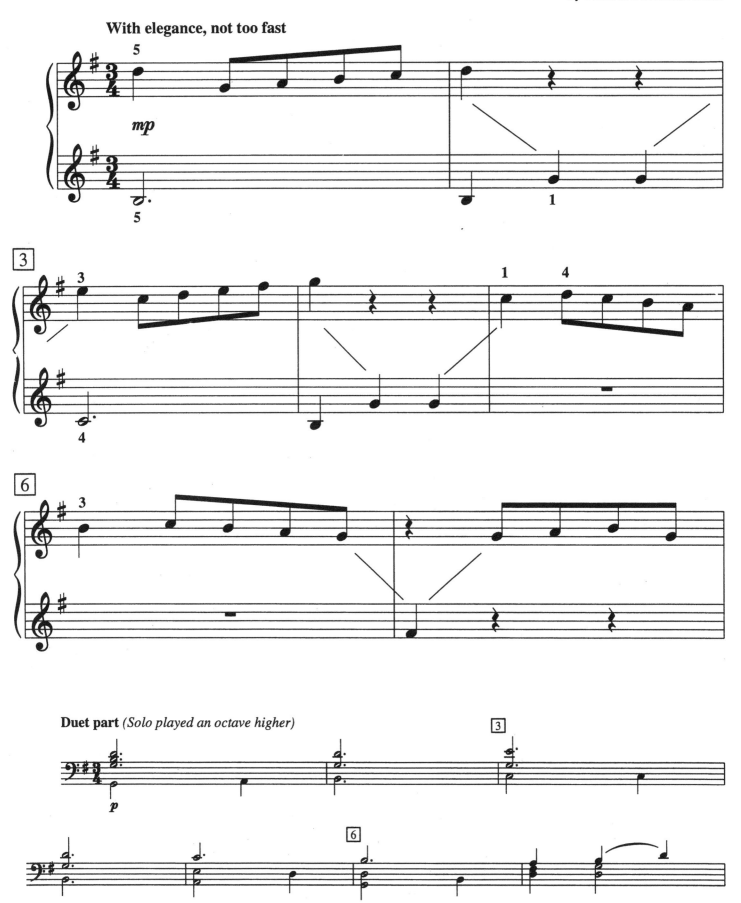

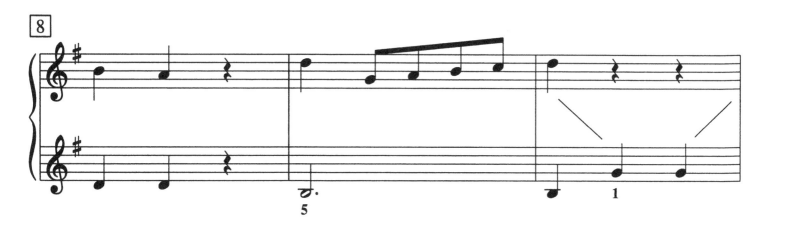

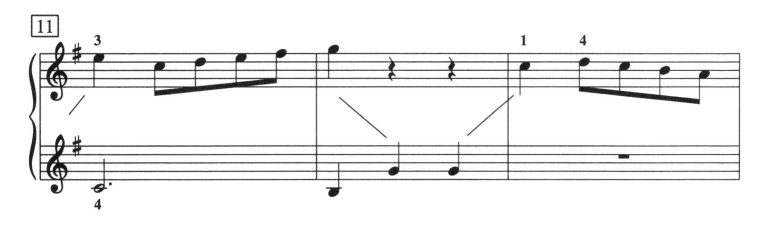

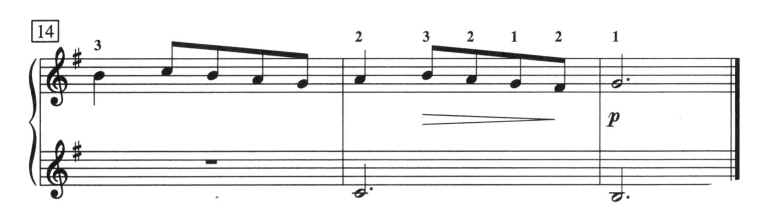

The Muffin Man

Traditional

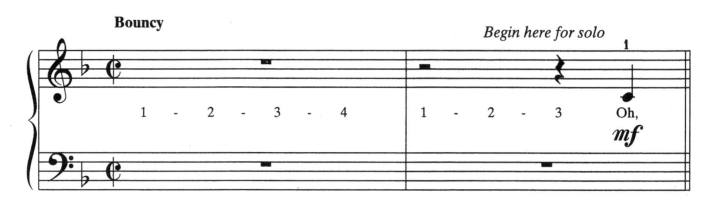

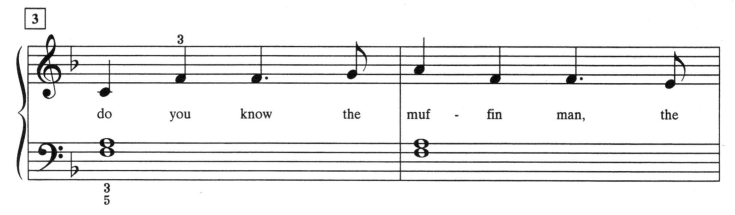

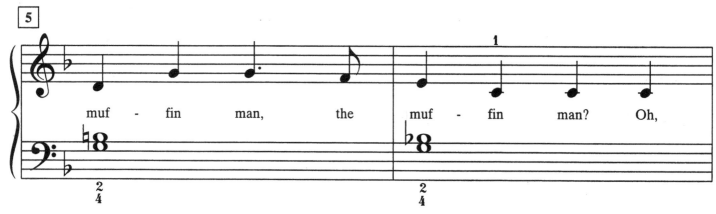

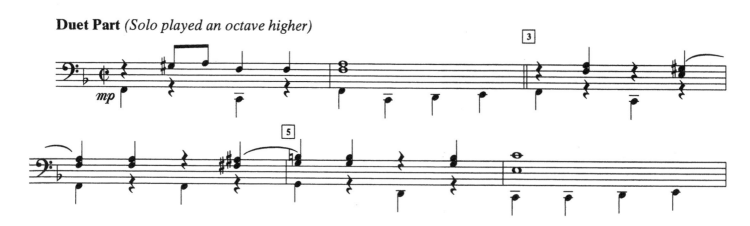

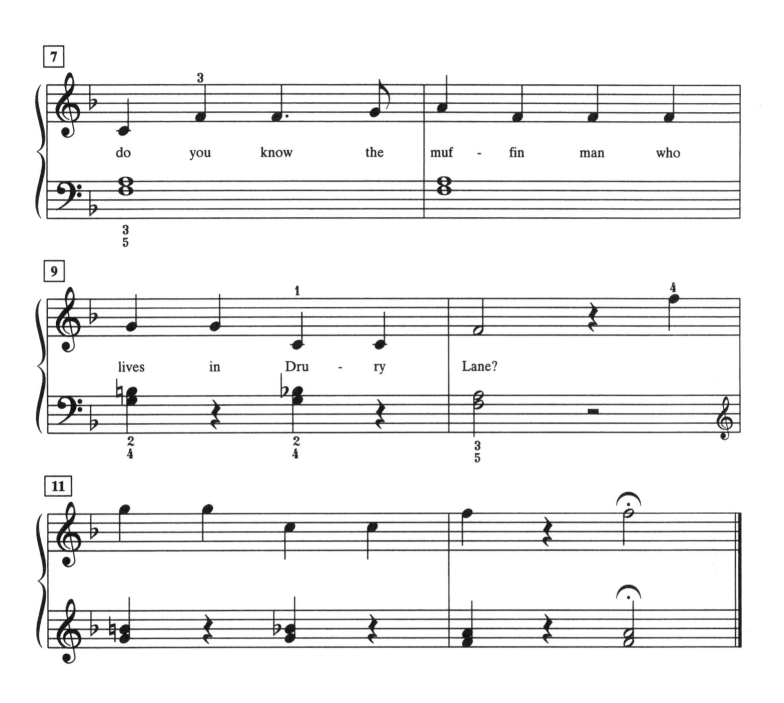

The Mulberry Bush

Traditional

Oh Where, Oh Where
Has My Little Dog Gone

Words by Sep. Winner

Traditional Melody

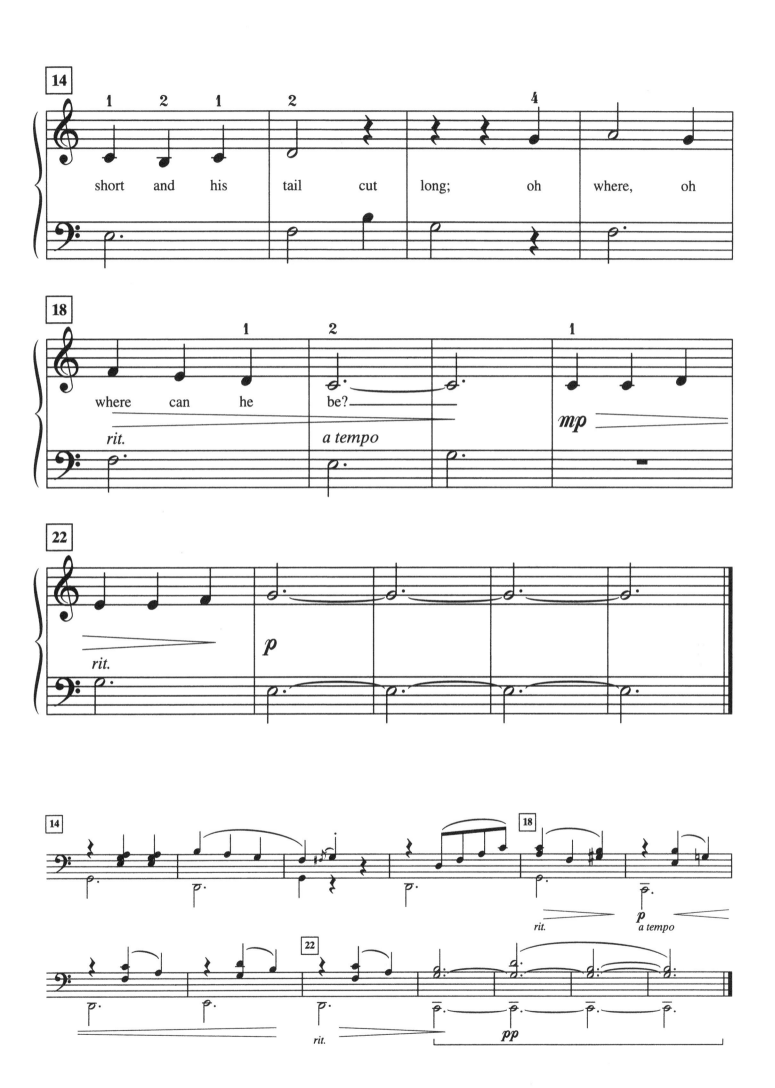

short   and   his   tail   cut   long;   oh   where,   oh

where   can   he   be?   _____   _____

rit.   a tempo

mp

rit.   *p*

Old MacDonald Had a Farm

Traditional

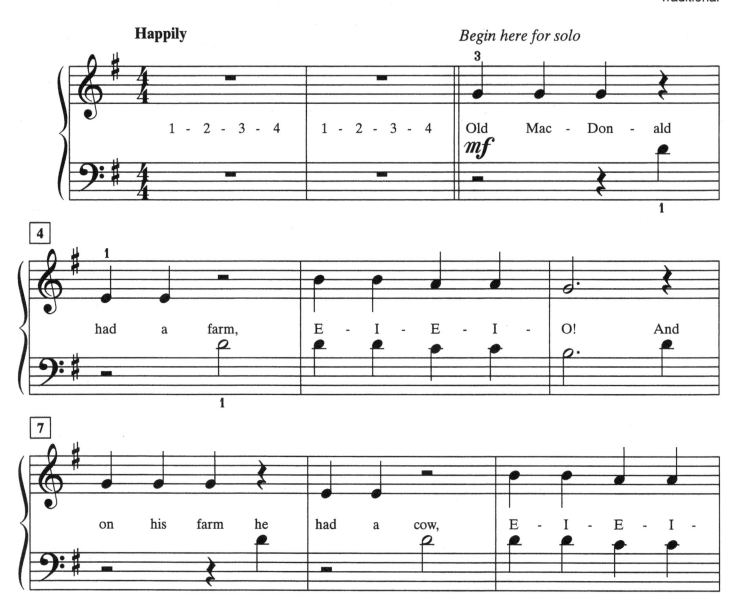

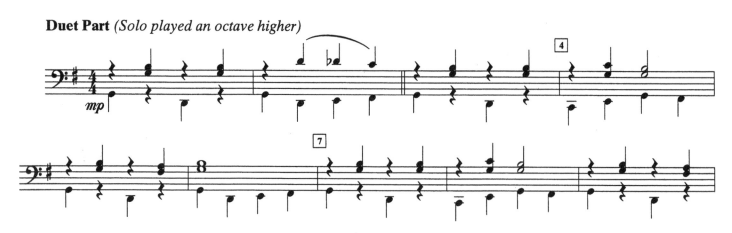

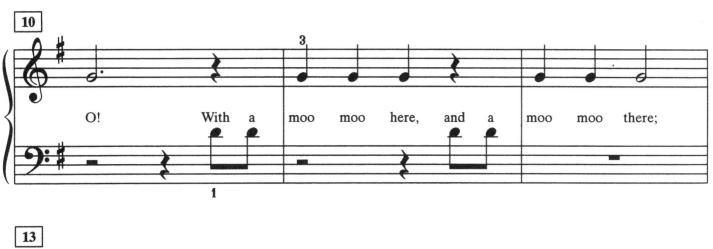

Over the River and Through the Woods

Traditional

Traveling along, moderately fast

O - ver the riv - er and through the woods, to
O - ver the riv - er and through the woods, oh

Grand - moth - er's house we go; the
how the wind does blow! It

horse knows the way to car - ry the sleigh, through the

Duet part *(Solo played an octave higher)*

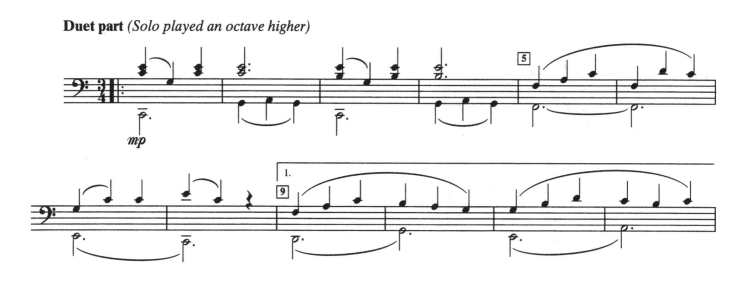

Pomp and Circumstance

By Edward Elgar

Slowly, with dignity

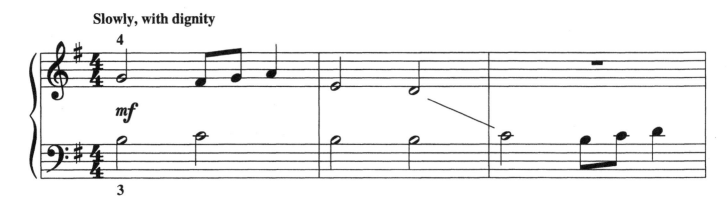

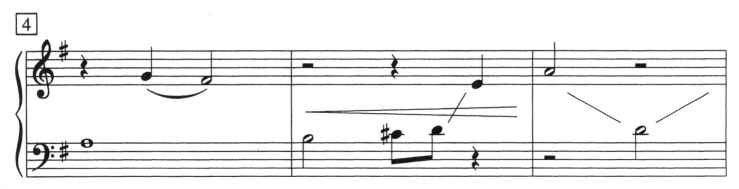

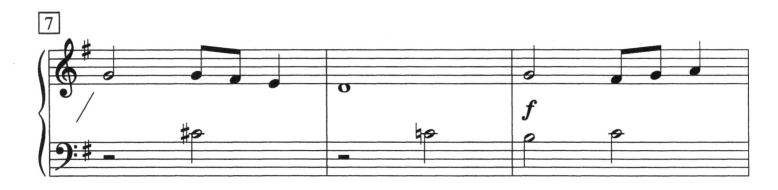

Duet part *(Solo played an octave higher)*

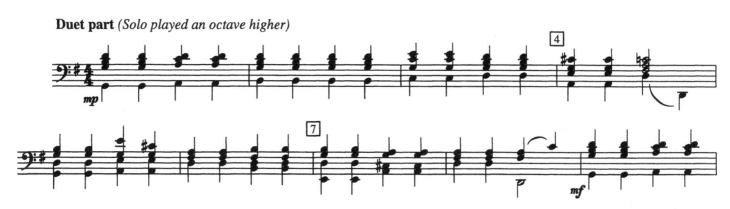

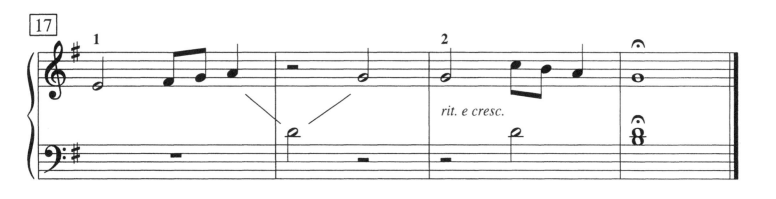

Pop Goes the Weasel

Traditional

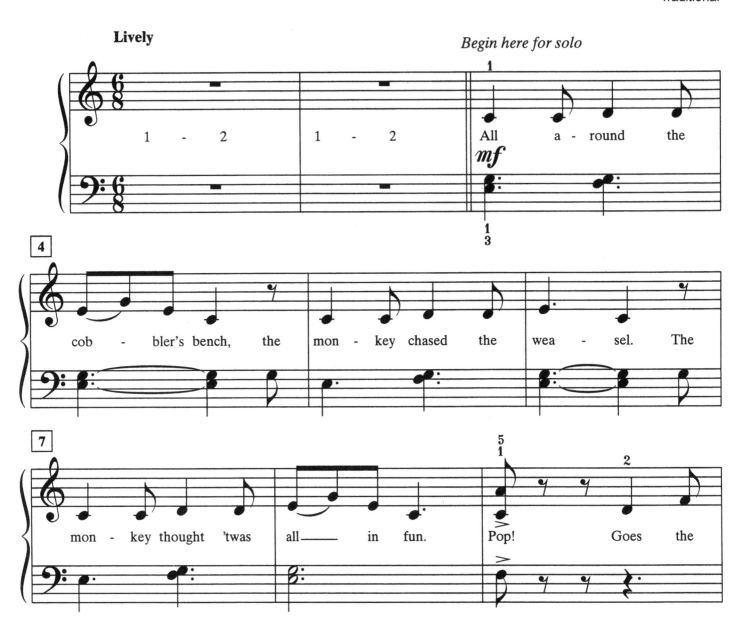

Duet Part *(Solo played an octave higher)*

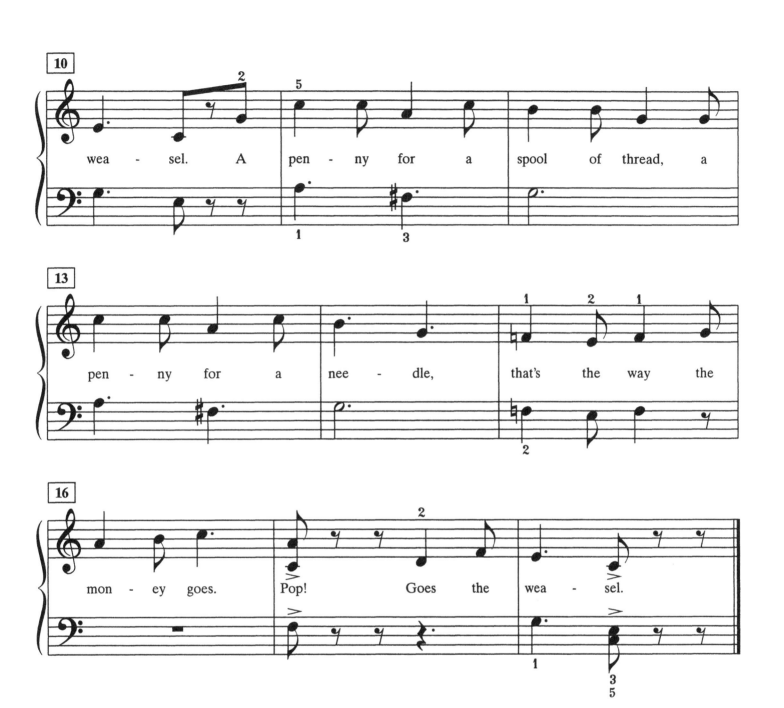

Puff the Magic Dragon

Words and Music by
Lenny Lipton and Peter Yarrow

Moderately, with expression

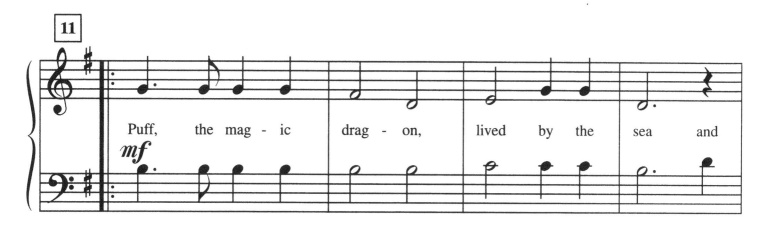

Puff, the mag - ic drag - on, lived by the sea and

frol- icked in the au - tumn mist in a land called Hon - a - lee.

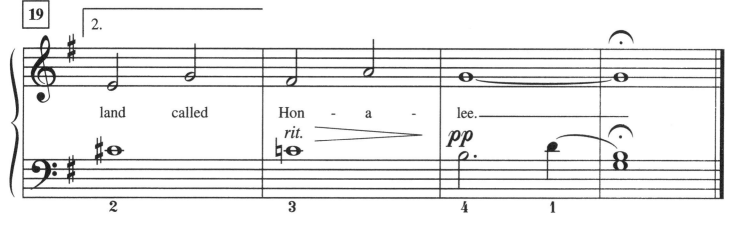

land called Hon - a - lee.

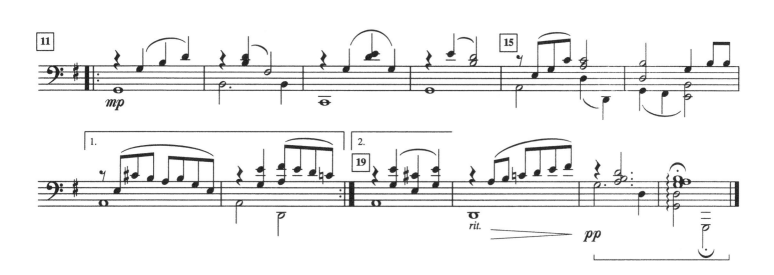

She'll Be Comin' 'Round the Mountain

Traditional

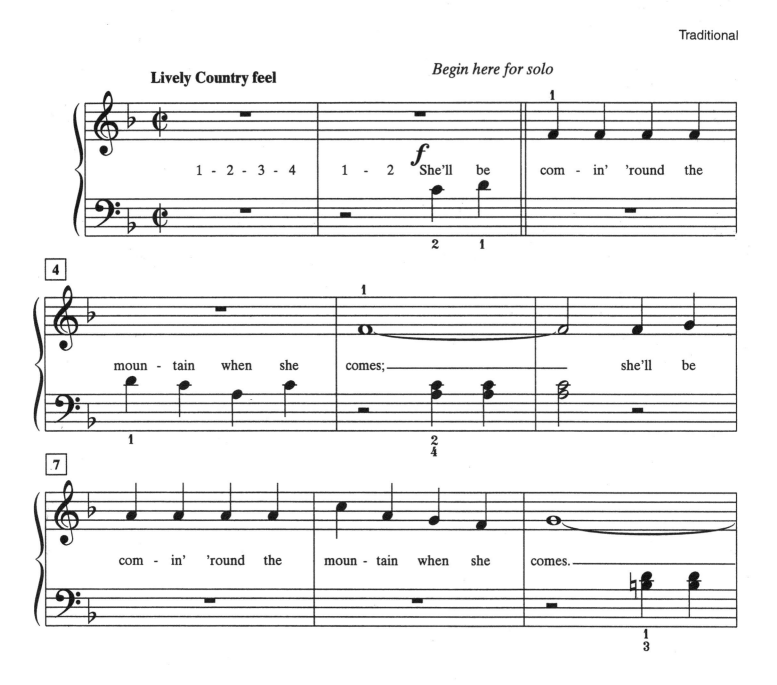

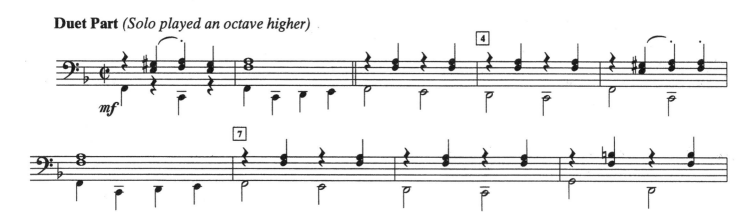

Silent Night

Words by Joseph Mohr
Translated by John F. Young

Music by Franz X. Gruber

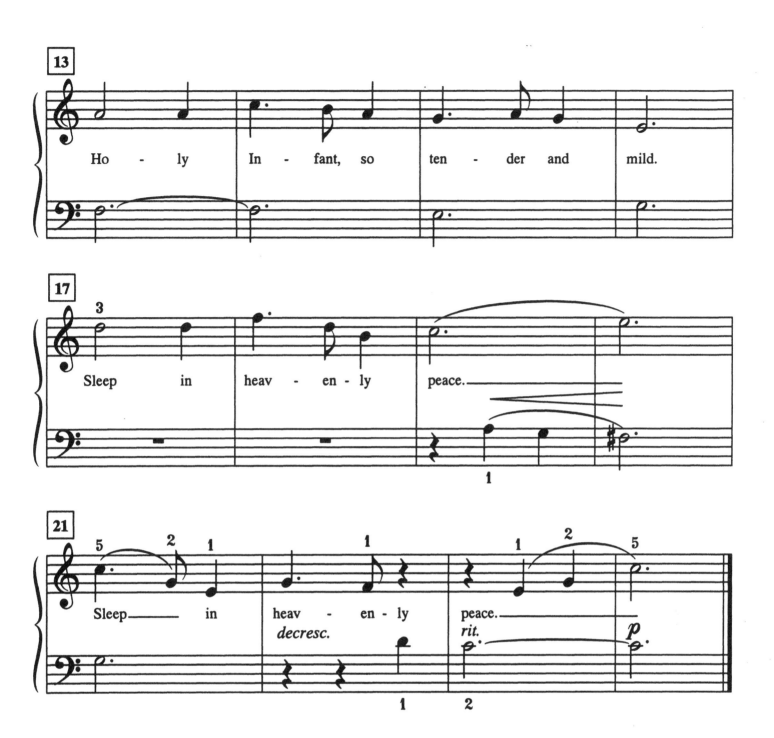

Sing a Song of Sixpence

Traditional

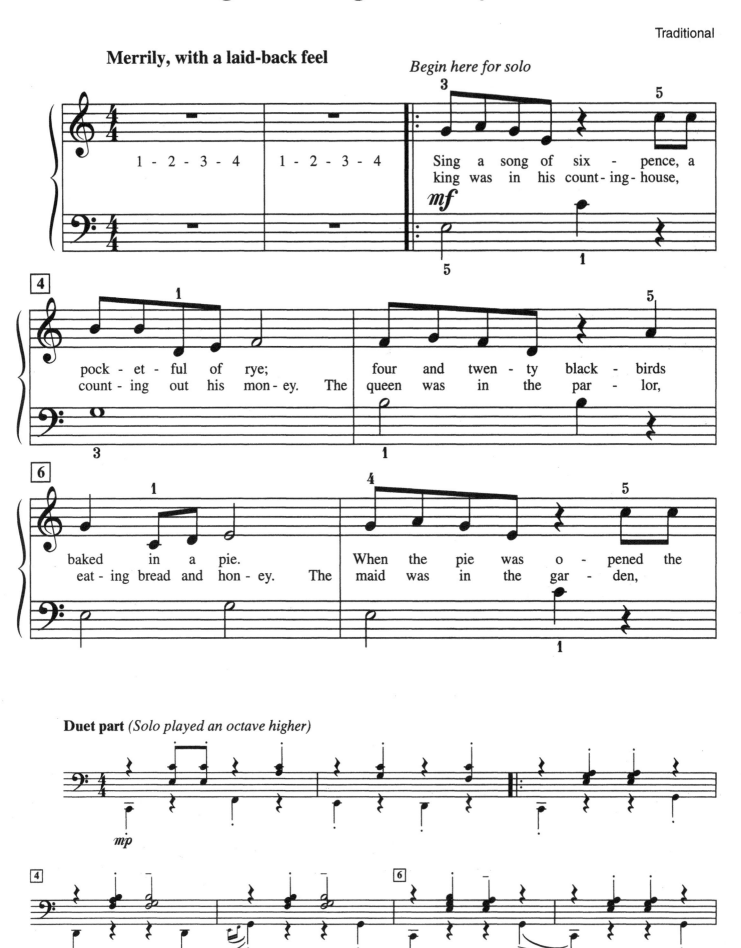

birds be - gan to sing.
hang - ing out the clothes. A -

Was - n't that a dain - ty thing to

set be - fore a king? The

long— came a black - bird and

pecked— off her nose.

The Skaters' Waltz

By Emil Waldteufel

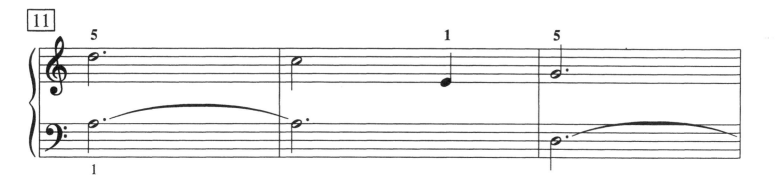

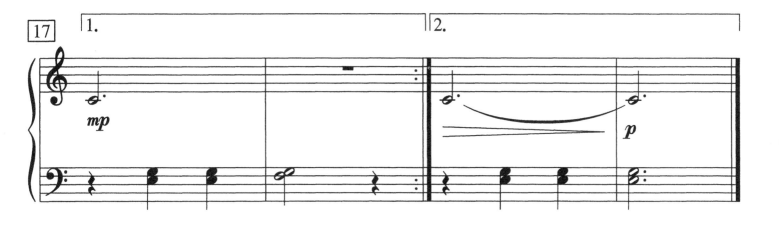

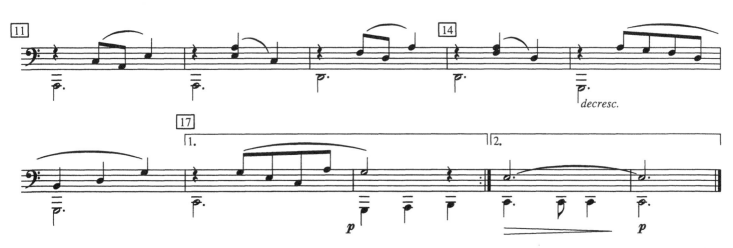

Skip to My Lou

Traditional

Duet part *(Solo played an octave higher)*

Someday Out of the Blue

(Theme from El Dorado)

from THE ROAD TO EL DORADO

Lyrics by Tim Rice

Music by Elton John and Patrick Leonard

Moderately, with expression

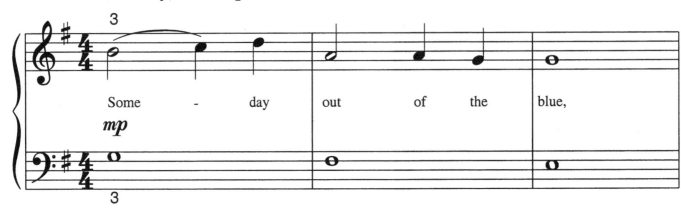

Some - day out of the blue,

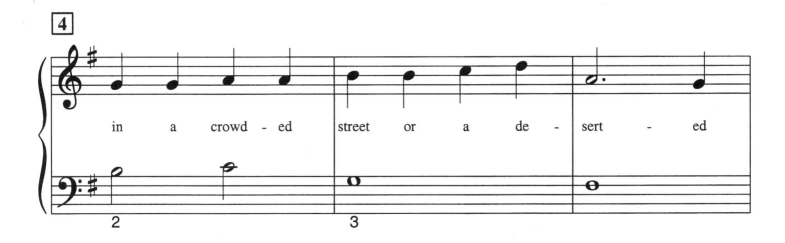

in a crowd - ed street or a de - sert - ed

Duet Part (*Solo played an octave higher*)

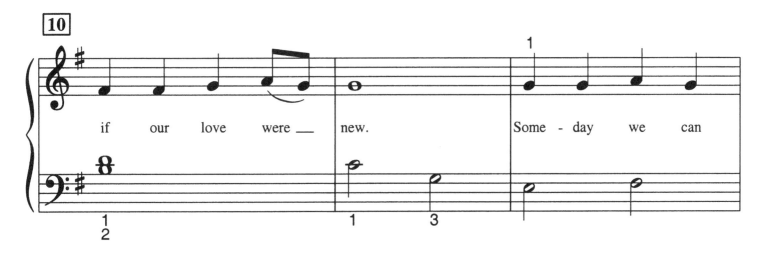

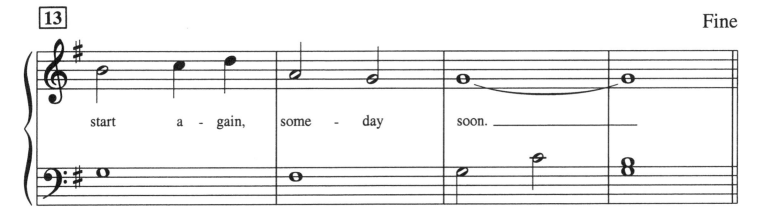

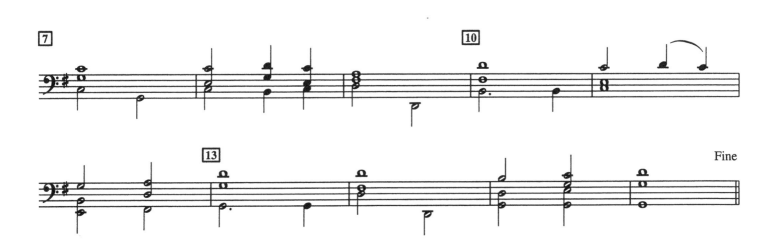

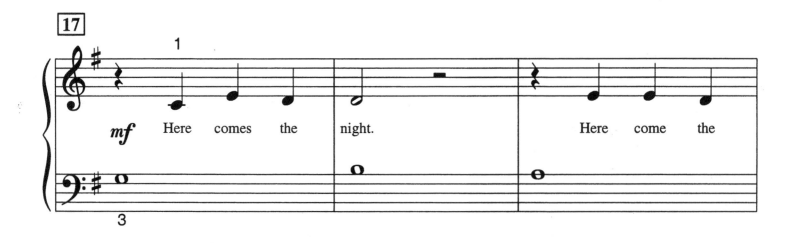

Here comes the night. Here come the

mem - o - ries. Lost in your arms,

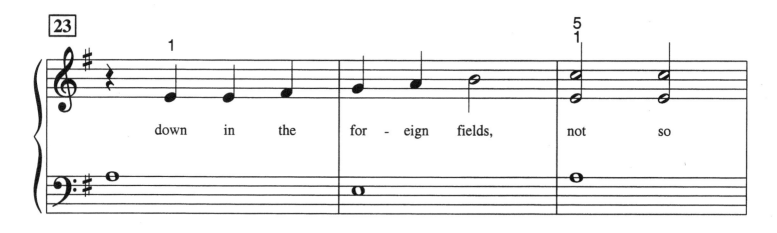

down in the for - eign fields, not so

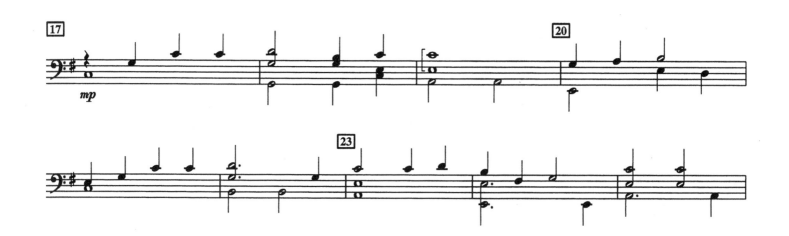

long a - go. Seems like e - ter - ni - ty.

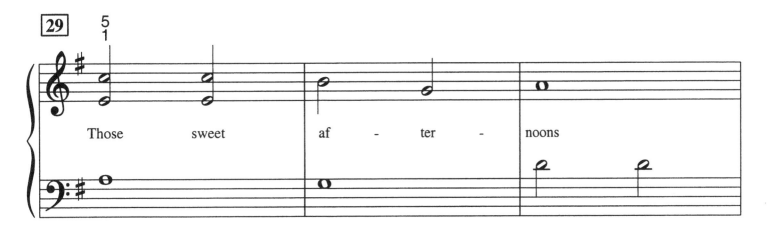

Those sweet af - ter - noons

D.C. al Fine

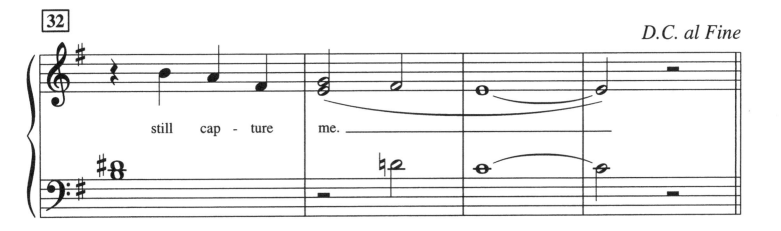

still cap - ture me.

D.C. al Fine

"Surprise" Symphony

By Franz Joseph Haydn

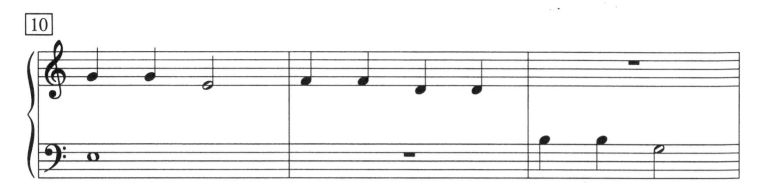

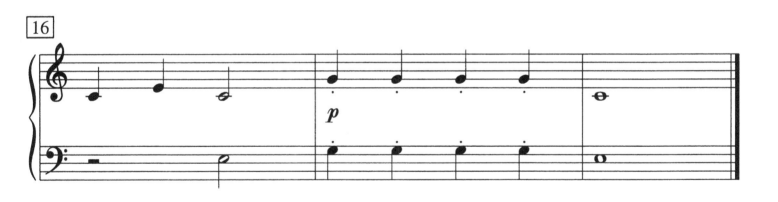

Ten Little Indians

Traditional

Big tom-tom beat

Begin here for solo

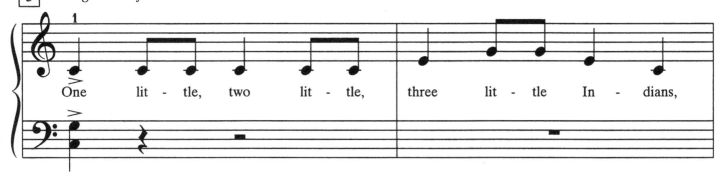

One lit - tle, two lit - tle, three lit - tle In - dians,

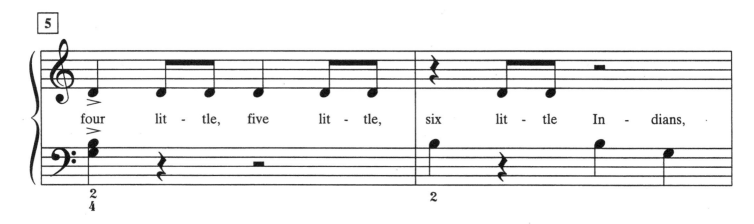

four lit - tle, five lit - tle, six lit - tle In - dians,

Duet Part *(Solo played an octave higher)*

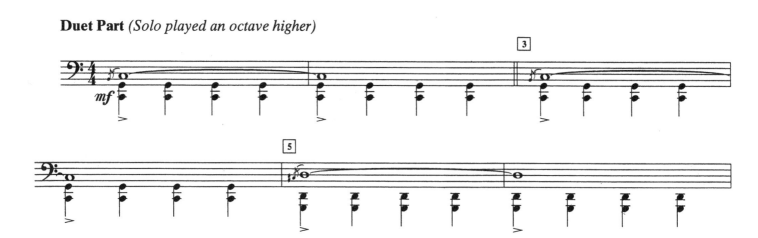

Thank You Very Much

from SCROOGE

Words and Music by
Leslie Bricusse

Duet Part *(Solo played an octave higher)*

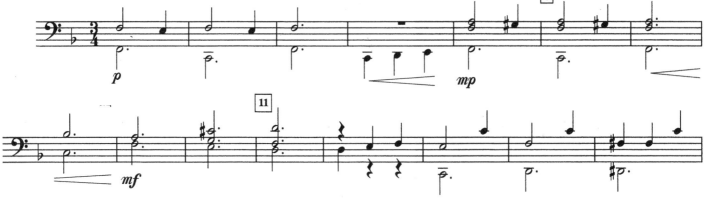

There Was an Old Woman
Who Lived in a Shoe

Traditional

This Old Man

Traditional

Light March

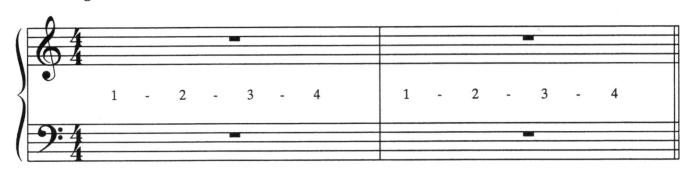

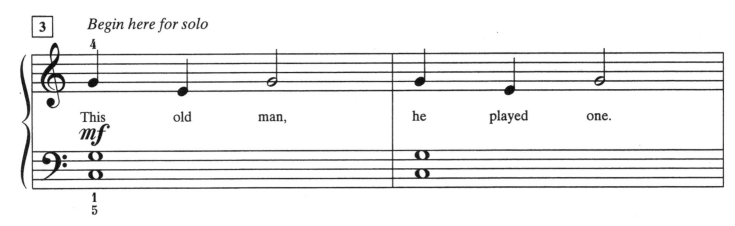

Duet Part *(Solo played an octave higher)*

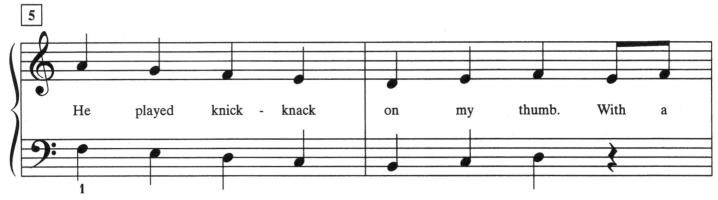

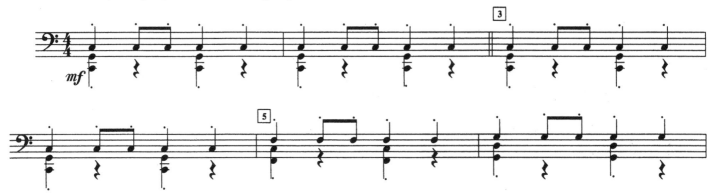

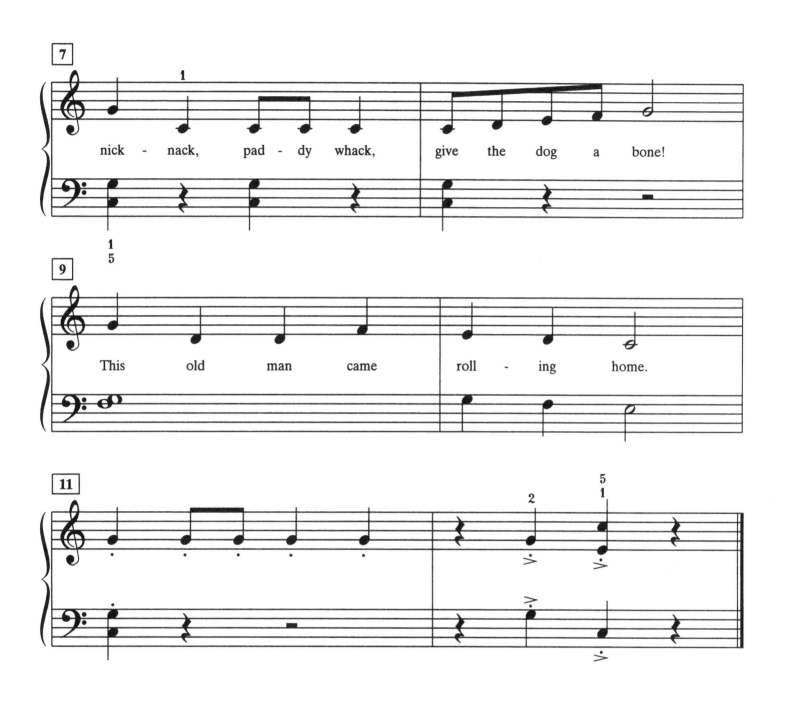

Twinkle, Twinkle Little Star

Traditional

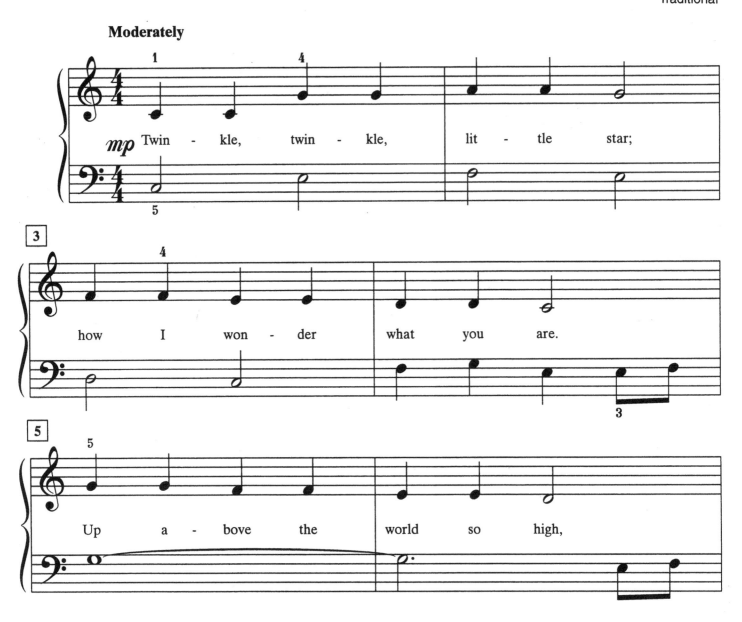

Duet Part *(Solo played an octave higher)*

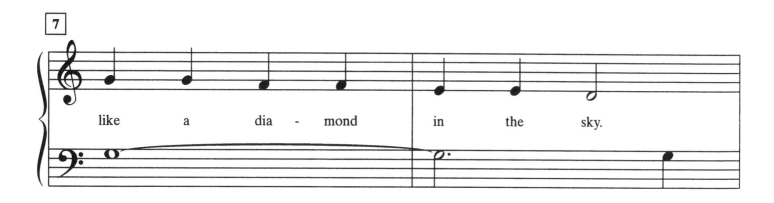

like a dia - mond in the sky.

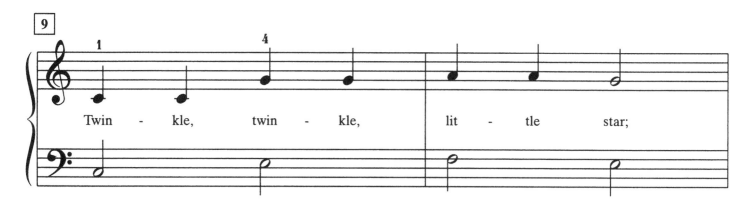

Twin - kle, twin - kle, lit - tle star;

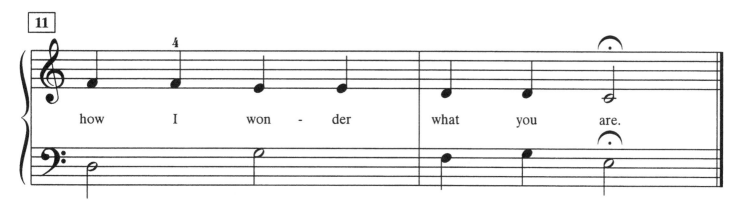

how I won - der what you are.

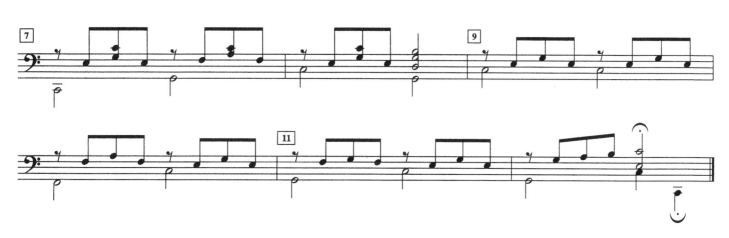

We Wish You a Merry Christmas

Traditional English Folksong

Lively Waltz tempo

Begin here for solo

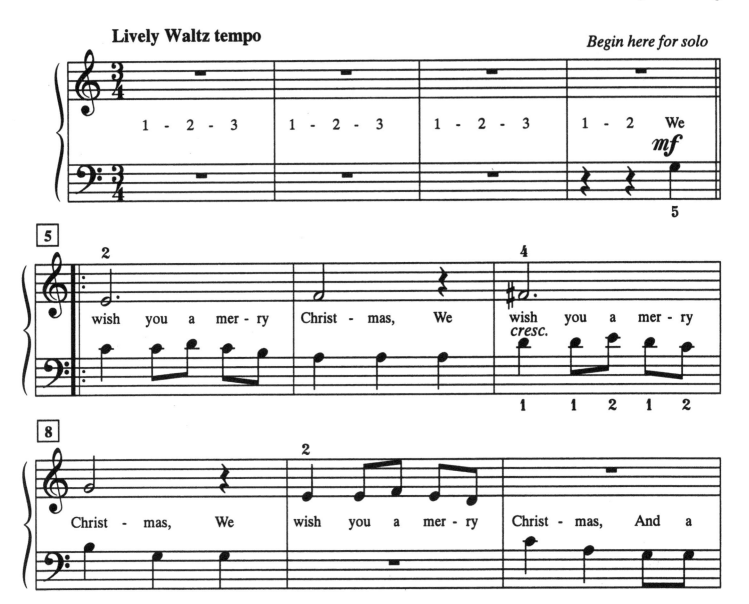

Duet Part *(Solo played an octave higher)*

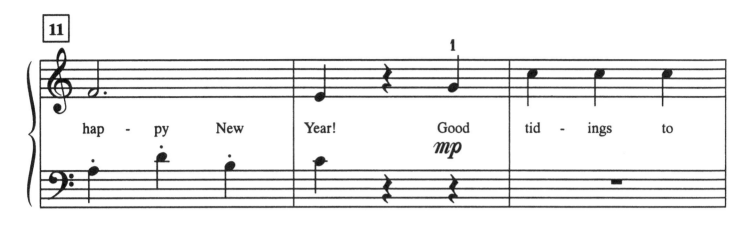

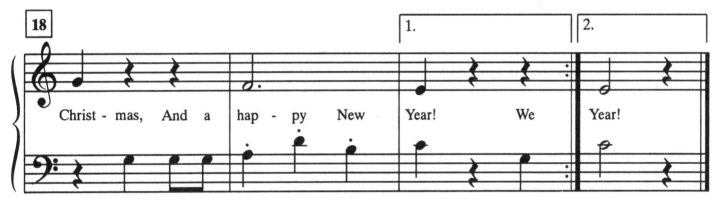

When You Believe

(From The Prince Of Egypt)
from THE PRINCE OF EGYPT

Words and Music Composed by Stephen Schwartz
with Additional Music by Babyface

Slowly

Man - y nights we've prayed, with no proof an - y - one could hear.
we are not a - fraid, al - though we know there's much to fear.

In our hearts a hope - ful song _ we bare - ly un - der - stood. Now
We were mov - ing moun - tains long _ be -

1.

2.
fore we knew we could. _

There can be mir - a - cles,
Who knows what mir - a - cles

Duet Part *(Solo played an octave higher)*

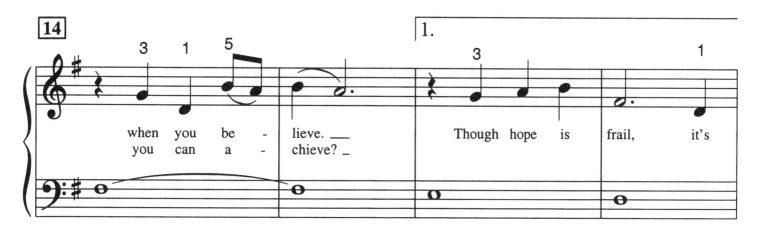

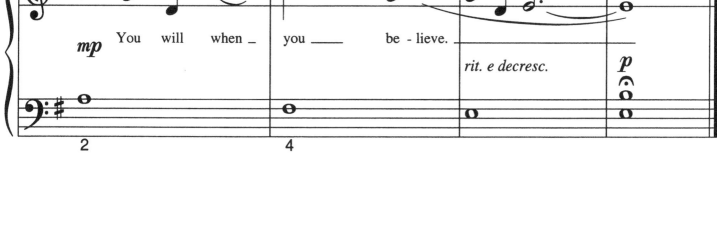

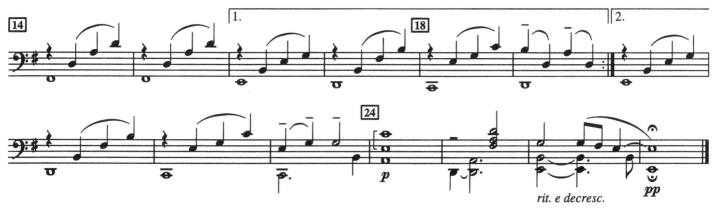

William Tell Overture

By G. Rossini

More Big-Note & Easy Piano Books

For a complete listing of Cherry Lane titles available, including contents listings, please visit our web site at www.cherrylaneprint.com

BEAUTIFUL POP BALLADS FOR EASY PIANO
31 lovely pop songs in simplified arrangements, including: Don't Know Why • From a Distance • Hero • Just Once • My Cherie Amour • November Rain • Open Arms • Time After Time • Unchained Melody • What a Wonderful World • Your Song • and more.
_____ 02502450 Easy Piano $12.99

CHOPIN FOR EASY PIANO
This special easy piano version features the composer's intricate melodies, harmonies and rhythms newly arranged so that virtually all pianists can experience the thrill of playing Chopin at the piano! Includes 20 favorites mazurkas, nocturnes, polonaises, preludes and waltzes.
_____ 02501483 Easy Piano $7.99

CLASSICAL CHRISTMAS
Easy solo arrangements of 30 wonderful holiday songs: Ave Maria • Dance of the Sugar Plum Fairy • Evening Prayer • Gesu Bambino • Hallelujah! • He Shall Feed His Flock • March of the Toys • O Come, All Ye Faithful • O Holy Night • Pastoral Symphony • Sheep May Safely Graze • Sinfonia • Waltz of the Flowers • and more.
_____ 02500112 Easy Piano Solo $9.95

BEST OF JOHN DENVER
A collection of 18 Denver classics, including: Leaving on a Jet Plane • Take Me Home, Country Roads • Rocky Mountain High • Follow Me • and more.
_____ 02505512 Easy Piano $9.95

JOHN DENVER ANTHOLOGY
Easy arrangements of 34 of the finest from this beloved artist. Includes: Annie's Song • Fly Away • Follow Me • Grandma's Feather Bed • Leaving on a Jet Plane • Perhaps Love • Rocky Mountain High • Sunshine on My Shoulders • Take Me Home, Country Roads • Thank God I'm a Country Boy • and many more.
_____ 02501366 Easy Piano $19.99

EASY BROADWAY SHOWSTOPPERS
Easy piano arrangements of 16 traditional and new Broadway standards, including: "Impossible Dream" from Man of La Mancha • "Unusual Way" from Nine • "This Is the Moment" from Jekyll & Hyde • many more.
_____ 02505517 Easy Piano $12.95

A FAMILY CHRISTMAS AROUND THE PIANO
25 songs for hours of family fun, including: Away in a Manger • Deck the Hall • The First Noel • God Rest Ye Merry, Gentlemen • Hark! the Herald Angels Sing • Jingle Bells • Jolly Old St. Nicholas • Joy to the World • O Little Town of Bethlehem • Silent Night, Holy Night • The Twelve Days of Christmas • and more.
_____ 02500398 Easy Piano $8.99

FAVORITE CELTIC SONGS FOR EASY PIANO
Easy arrangements of 40 Celtic classics, including: The Ash Grove • The Bluebells of Scotland • A Bunch of Thyme • Danny Boy • Finnegan's Wake • I'll Tell Me Ma • Loch Lomond • My Wild Irish Rose • The Rose of Tralee • and more!
_____ 02501306 Easy Piano $12.99

HOLY CHRISTMAS CAROLS COLORING BOOK
A terrific songbook with 7 sacred carols and lots of coloring pages for the young pianist. Songs include: Angels We Have Heard on High • The First Noel • Hark! The Herald Angels Sing • It Came upon a Midnight Clear • O Come All Ye Faithful • O Little Town of Bethlehem • Silent Night.
_____ 02500277 Five-Finger Piano $6.95

JEKYLL & HYDE – VOCAL SELECTIONS
Ten songs from the Wildhorn/Bricusse Broadway smash, arranged for big-note: In His Eyes • It's a Dangerous Game • Lost in the Darkness • A New Life • No One Knows Who I Am • Once Upon a Dream • Someone Like You • Sympathy, Tenderness • Take Me as I Am • This Is the Moment.
_____ 02500023 Big-Note Piano................................. $9.95

JACK JOHNSON ANTHOLOGY
Easy arrangements of 27 of the best from this Hawaiian singer/songwriter, including: Better Together • Breakdown • Flake • Fortunate Fool • Good People • Sitting, Waiting, Wishing • Taylor • and more.
_____ 02501313 Easy Piano $19.99

JUST FOR KIDS – NOT! CHRISTMAS SONGS
This unique collection of 14 Christmas favorites is fun for the whole family! Kids can play the full-sounding big-note solos alone, or with their parents (or teachers) playing accompaniment for the thrill of four-hand piano! Includes: Deck the Halls • Jingle Bells • Silent Night • What Child Is This? • and more.
_____ 02505510 Big-Note Piano................................. $8.95

JUST FOR KIDS – NOT! CLASSICS
Features big-note arrangements of classical masterpieces, plus optional accompaniment for adults. Songs: Air on the G String • Dance of the Sugar Plum Fairy • Für Elise • Jesu, Joy of Man's Desiring • Ode to Joy • Pomp and Circumstance • The Sorcerer's Apprentice • William Tell Overture • and more!
_____ 02505513 Classics... $7.95
_____ 02500301 More Classics $8.95

JUST FOR KIDS – NOT! FUN SONGS
Fun favorites for kids everywhere in big-note arrangements for piano, including: Bingo • Eensy Weensy Spider • Farmer in the Dell • Jingle Bells • London Bridge • Pop Goes the Weasel • Puff the Magic Dragon • Skip to My Lou • Twinkle, Twinkle Little Star • and more!
_____ 02505523 Fun Songs $7.95

JUST FOR KIDS – NOT! TV THEMES & MOVIE SONGS
Entice the kids to the piano with this delightful collection of songs and themes from movies and TV. These big-note arrangements include themes from The Brady Bunch and The Addams Family, as well as Do-Re-Mi (The Sound of Music), theme from Beetlejuice (Day-O) and Puff the Magic Dragon. Each song includes an accompaniment part for teacher or adult so that the kids can experience the joy of four-hand playing as well! Plus performance tips.
_____ 02505507 TV Themes & Movie Songs.............................. $9.95
_____ 02500304 More TV Themes & Movie Songs $9.95

BEST OF JOHN MAYER FOR EASY PIANO
15 of Mayer's best arranged for easy piano, including: Daughters • Gravity • My Stupid Mouth • No Such Thing • Waiting on the World to Change • Who Says • Why Georgia • Your Body Is a Wonderland • and more.
_____ 02501705 Easy Piano $16.99

POKEMON 2 B.A. MASTER
This great songbook features easy piano arrangements of 13 tunes from the hit TV series: 2.B.A. Master • Double Trouble (Team Rocket) • Everything Changes • Misty's Song • My Best Friends • Pokémon (Dance Mix) • Pokémon Theme • PokéRAP • The Time Has Come (Pikachu's Goodbye) • Together, Forever • Viridian City • What Kind of Pokémon Are You? • You Can Do It (If You Really Try). Includes a full-color, 8-page pull-out section featuring characters and scenes from this super hot show.
_____ 02500145 Easy Piano $12.95

POPULAR CHRISTMAS CAROLS COLORING BOOK
Kids are sure to love this fun holiday songbook! It features five-finger piano arrangements of seven Christmas classics, complete with coloring pages throughout! Songs include: Deck the Hall • Good King Wenceslas • Jingle Bells • Jolly Old St. Nicholas • O Christmas Tree • Up on the Housetop • We Wish You a Merry Christmas.
_____ 02500276 Five-Finger Piano $6.95

PUFF THE MAGIC DRAGON & 54 OTHER ALL-TIME CHILDREN'S FAVORITESONGS
55 timeless songs enjoyed by generations of kids, and sure to be favorites for years to come. Songs include: A-Tisket A-Tasket • Alouette • Eensy Weensy Spider • The Farmer in the Dell • I've Been Working on the Railroad • If You're Happy and You Know It • Joy to the World • Michael Finnegan • Oh Where, Oh Where Has My Little Dog Gone • Silent Night • Skip to My Lou • This Old Man • and many more.
_____ 02500017 Big-Note Piano.. $12.95